DECORATING WITH GREAT FINDS

82 Ways to Use Finds from Antique Stores, Garage Sales & Attics

The Home Decorating Institute®

Copyright © 1995 Cy DeCosse Incorporated 5900 Green Oak Drive Minnetonka, Minnesota 55343
1-800-328-3895 All rights reserved Printed in U.S.A.

Library of Congress Cataloging-in-Publication Data Decorating with great finds / Home Decorating Institute.
p. cm. — (Arts & crafts for home decorating) Includes index. ISBN 0-86573-382-1. — ISBN 0-86573-383-X (softcover) 1. House
furnishings—Recycling. 2. Household linens—Recycling. 3. Furniture finishing. 4. Windows—Recycling. 5. Doors—Recycling.
6. Found objects (Art) in interior decoration. I. Home Decorating Institute (Minnetonka, Minn.) II. Cy DeCosse Incorporated.
III. Series.   TT149.D43 1995 645—dc20   95-2318

CONTENTS

Decorating with Great Finds

Refurbishing

New Uses for Old Finds

Found Fabrics

Displaying Great Finds

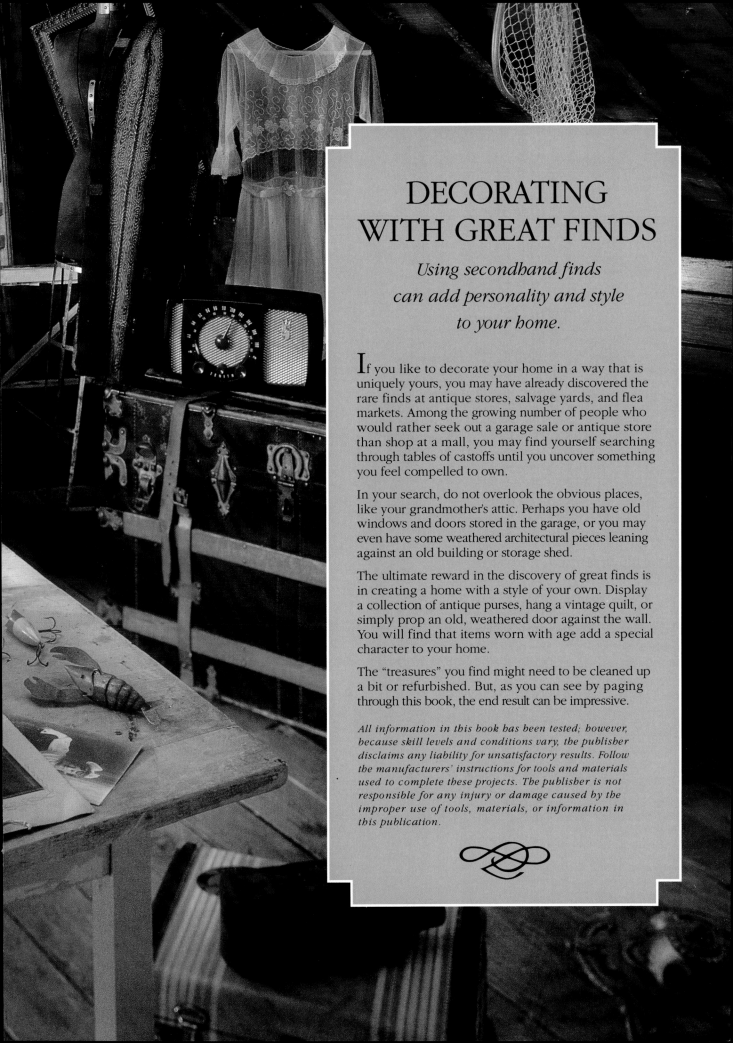

DECORATING WITH GREAT FINDS

*Using secondhand finds
can add personality and style
to your home.*

If you like to decorate your home in a way that is uniquely yours, you may have already discovered the rare finds at antique stores, salvage yards, and flea markets. Among the growing number of people who would rather seek out a garage sale or antique store than shop at a mall, you may find yourself searching through tables of castoffs until you uncover something you feel compelled to own.

In your search, do not overlook the obvious places, like your grandmother's attic. Perhaps you have old windows and doors stored in the garage, or you may even have some weathered architectural pieces leaning against an old building or storage shed.

The ultimate reward in the discovery of great finds is in creating a home with a style of your own. Display a collection of antique purses, hang a vintage quilt, or simply prop an old, weathered door against the wall. You will find that items worn with age add a special character to your home.

The "treasures" you find might need to be cleaned up a bit or refurbished. But, as you can see by paging through this book, the end result can be impressive.

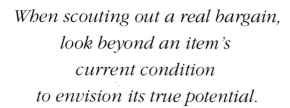

BUYING WITH A VISION

*When scouting out a real bargain,
look beyond an item's
current condition
to envision its true potential.*

Balusters *discovered in a salvage
yard can become candlesticks
(page 64).*

In your search for great finds, do not discount old stained glass windows in need of a little refurbishing, an antique footstool that needs new upholstery, or a trunk with damaged hardware or a torn lining. These items are all easily renovated. At first glance, you may not even consider buying a picture frame if the carved wood is chipped or if the finish does not suit you. However, using a few simple techniques, you can repair the wood carvings and revitalize the frame with a gold-leaf finish. And, once restored, the classic frame fits beautifully into a traditional home.

Some items can be used for decorating the home without any renovations necessary. Collections are frequently displayed in "as is" condition. Weathered architectural pieces with crackled or aged paint finishes can fit right in with the distressed wood furniture of a country home. Timeworn items can contrast sharply with contemporary furnishings to create instant impact.

Sometimes a found object can be improved by changing its finish, perhaps in keeping with the aged look of the piece. Worn, weathered, rusted, scrubbed, verdigris, and crackled finishes can all be duplicated in a few easy steps.

Ordinary items can be used creatively to add a new twist to your decorating. Consider transforming a discarded door into a coffee table. Or use salvaged shutters to build a corner shelf, and make a tiered serving tray from old plates.

Weathered oar (above) found leaning against an old boat house is kept in its aged condition by preserving the finish (page 26). Used as a curtain rod (below), the oar lends an element of surprise to the room.

Picture frame with beautiful detailing was found at an antique store at a modest price. However, the original gold leaf was painted over by its second owner, and the carved wood was chipped. To restore the frame, the wood carvings have been repaired (page 16) and a gold-leaf finish with an aged look (page 28) has been applied.

FOUND:
OLD WINDOWS,
DOORS &
SHUTTERS

Windows, doors, and shutters are often found at salvage yards and antique stores. But, often, you need not look any farther than your own garage. Items that have nicely weathered finishes may be used in their existing condition or may be repainted in any desired finish for a newer look. Used in creative ways, these old items can take on new life.

Bench *is created from a narrow door, as on page 56, using the top and bottom of the door as the legs of the bench.*

Tabletop display *consists of several shutters in an interesting arrangement.*

Mirror *(left) is created from a unique old window as on page 51.*

Pot rack, made from an interesting window with a weathered finish, as on page 54, adds character to a country kitchen.

Desk in a traditional library setting consists of an old door supported on Ionic columns. The door is covered with a glass top, to provide a smooth writing surface.

Kitchen rack (right) is simply an old shutter hung on the wall. S-hooks are used to hang the utensils from the shutter.

FOUND: OLD FABRICS

Attics and antique stores are often filled with old linens, tapestries, handmade quilts, and needlework as well as wedding gowns, christening gowns, and other cherished garments. These lovely textile items, whether they are used intact or made into pillows and other room accessories, add character and style to any decorating scheme.

Feed bag pillow with a quilt border (page 89) makes a clever accessory in a country room. The cotton fabrics are softly faded due to aging, adding to the nostalgic look.

Wall hanging, sewn as on page 100, shows off the beauty of a traditional tapestry. For more impact, the wall hanging is framed with a border and accented with trims.

Vintage kitchen towels (left) in an assortment of styles create a unique display when hung on an old ladder.

Embroidered tablecloth *is draped softly at the top of a window, for an easy, no-sew swag.*

Collection of small purses, *embellished with beading and needlework, create a lovely wall grouping.*

Vintage kimono *makes a bold statement in a contemporary setting.*

Antique garments, *such as the delicate example at right, can be creatively displayed by hanging them from a clothesline near the ceiling.*

FOUND:
OLD MEMORABILIA

Cherished heirlooms, such as an old family trunk and Grandfather's favorite fishing equipment, can hold an important place in the home. Family photographs, which can be preserved with special conservation framing techniques, can also be proudly displayed.

Handed-down collectibles *(right) are mounted on lamp bases to show them off. Lamps are easily assembled (page 71) by using figurine arms and other basic lamp parts.*

Grandfather's fishing gear *(below) is preserved in a shadow box (page 115) as a pleasant reminder of family outings.*

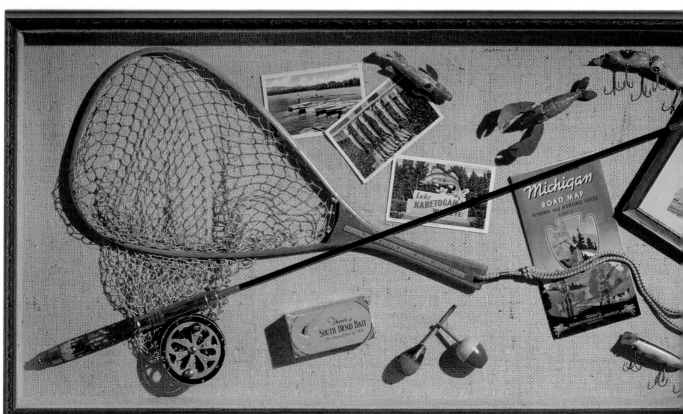

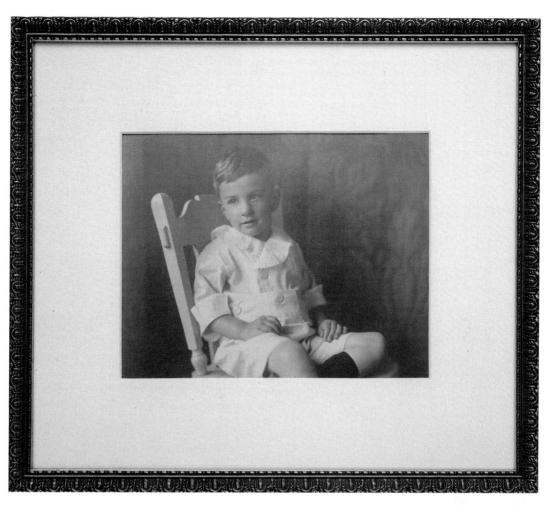

Cherished photograph is preserved for generations to come, using conservation framing methods (page 104).

Old trunks have been renovated (page 34) by replacing the straps and hardware and adding new linings.

Refurbishing

REPAIRING CARVED WOOD

Many old wooden pieces are beautifully crafted with intricate carvings, and some pieces of molded plaster have fine detail work that replicates these carvings. Although portions of the carvings or details may be broken off, the item can frequently be repaired and refinished, using water putty.

Apply the water putty to the surface to be repaired, building up the putty slightly larger than the original carvings, to allow for sanding and shaping. When the putty is dry, use a file or 100-grit sandpaper to shape the replacement piece so it matches the original piece. For more intricate carvings, use wood-carver's tools to shape the piece.

MATERIALS

- Water putty.
- File or 100-grit sandpaper; wood-carver's tools, for intricate carvings.
- Tack cloth.
- Paint, stain, or other desired finish.

HOW TO REPAIR CARVED WOOD

1 Clean the item thoroughly, removing any loose chips of wood.

2 Mix the water putty according to the manufacturer's directions. Apply putty to the surface to be rebuilt, shaping it to resemble the original shape; build up putty slightly larger than the original carvings, to allow for sanding and shaping.

3 Allow putty to dry. Shape rebuilt area, using a file or 100-grit sandpaper. For more intricate carvings, use wood-carver's tools to shape the piece. Remove any grit, using a tack cloth.

4 Apply the desired finish, using paint or stain; test stain colors on a sample of dried water putty. For an aged look, apply one of the finishes on pages 22 to 31.

PRESERVING AGED FINISHES

Often the items you find at antique stores and salvage yards have timeworn finishes that add to their character and charm. These pieces have either been weathered through years of exposure to the elements or worn down through the wear-and-tear of constant use. Rather than trying to restore these aged pieces to their original finishes, you may prefer to leave them as they are, appreciating their history.

In many cases, all that is needed before displaying the aged items in your home is a good cleanup and, perhaps, a coat of beeswax to enliven an existing finish. Or apply an aerosol acrylic sealer or clear finish to seal the finish or add durability. By applying a beeswax, sealer, or clear finish, you can also prevent crackled or chipped paint from continually peeling, or prevent rust or verdigris from coming off onto your hands and clothing. Keep in mind that lead paints were used on most of the old pieces. To prevent the ingestion of any lead paint, consider how you plan to use old painted items in your decorating, and keep them away from children.

Weathered finish (above) has thinning layers of paint, and the bare wood is exposed in some areas, because of exposure to the elements. Preserve the finish with beeswax or a clear acrylic finish.

Crackled finish (left) has a random texture caused by the expansion and contraction of the surface when paint is brittle and old. When brittle paint cracks, the layers underneath are exposed, sometimes down to the bare wood. Preserve the finish with beeswax or a clear acrylic finish.

Worn finish (*right*) on painted or varnished wood shows aging in certain areas of use, such as near door handles and edges. Constantly used pieces from old farmhouses often have this type of aged finish. Preserve the finish with beeswax or a clear acrylic finish.

Scrubbed finish (*below*) has been subjected to the elements so long that the wood is completely devoid of paint or stain, exposing the bare wood. Preserve the finish with beeswax or a clear acrylic finish.

(Continued)

PRESERVING AGED
FINISHES (CONTINUED)

Verdigris finish shows the effects of aging on copper, brass, and bronze, resulting in various shades of green and blue. Preserve the finish by applying an aerosol clear acrylic sealer.

Rusted finish on metal has an interesting range of colors and a textural look. Preserve the finish by applying a rust-inhibiting aerosol clear acrylic sealer.

HOW TO PRESERVE WEATHERED, CRACKLED, WORN, OR SCRUBBED FINISHES

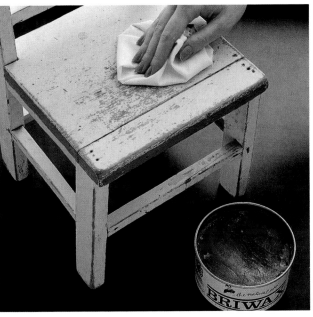

1 Beeswax method. Clean the surface with a solution of equal parts of vinegar and water, using a soft cloth; flaking paint will be removed. For removing stubborn stains, rub surface gently with a scouring pad; use old toothbrush in small areas. Allow to dry for several hours.

2 Apply beeswax generously to soft, lint-free cloth; rub beeswax onto surface. Then buff the wax by rubbing vigorously, using a clean, soft, lint-free cloth. Reapply and buff beeswax three times for a soft luster.

HOW TO PRESERVE A RUSTED OR VERDIGRIS FINISH

Clear finish method. Clean surface as in step 1, above. Apply clear acrylic finish, using a sponge applicator or natural-bristle paintbrush. Apply three coats; allow each to dry before recoating.

Clean surface as in step 1, above. Apply a light coat of aerosol clear acrylic sealer; if preserving a rusted finish, use a rust-inhibiting sealer, to prevent further rusting. Allow to dry. For good coverage, repeat three or four times, allowing sealer to dry between coats. The sealer prevents rust or verdigris from coming off onto hands and clothing; the verdigris may darken somewhat.

DUPLICATING AGED FINISHES

Scrubbed finish is duplicated by removing the paint with a wire brush or sandpaper and applying beeswax for a subtle sheen.

When you are shopping at antique stores, salvage yards, or garage sales, you will often find items that have wonderful detailing, but the finishes lack character or interest. The paint may be slightly chipped but not worn to the extent that you would like. Or someone may have even applied a fresh coat of paint to a wonderful old item, but you were looking for a piece that was weathered or worn.

Although you may prefer the authenticity of finishes that have aged on their own, aged finishes can be duplicated quite realistically. By duplicating an aged finish, you can select an old item for its style and detailing, rather than discounting it because the finish is not what you hoped for. In addition to the aged finishes shown here, the gold-leaf finish found on expensive antique picture frames and sconces can also be duplicated (page 28).

Before using any of the finishes, test the technique on a hidden area or on a scrap of a similar material, to become familiar with the process and to determine the effect you want to achieve.

Distressed wood, or the nicks and indentations in the wood on many old items, also contributes to the aged effect. If the piece you have is not as distressed as you would like it to be, you may distress the wood yourself as on page 24 before applying a finish. And decorative wood pieces with broken carvings may be repaired as on page 16.

Rusted finish is duplicated by painting the item black and then applying burnt sienna paint with a sea sponge.

Weathered finish is duplicated by applying paint to the item, allowing it to partially dry, and then removing some of it under running water.

Verdigris finish is duplicated by painting the item black and then applying aqua paint with a sea sponge.

Crackled finish is duplicated by applying a base coat of paint, a crackle medium, and a contrasting top coat of paint. Crackle medium makes the top coat crackle.

Worn finish is duplicated by applying paint to the item and then wiping it with a dampened rag to remove the paint in the areas that are normally subjected to wear.

HOW TO DISTRESS WOOD

1 Hit the wood with a hammer, chisel, and chain; pound holes randomly into the wood, using an awl. Make as many indentations and imperfections as desired.

2 Complete distressed look by chiseling edges randomly and rounding them off, using 100-grit sandpaper.

HOW TO DUPLICATE A WORN FINISH

MATERIALS

- Latex or acrylic paint.
- Sandpaper; tack cloth; clean, lint-free rag.

- Beeswax, clear acrylic finish, or aerosol clear acrylic sealer.

1 Clean surface to remove any grease and dirt. Rinse with clear water; allow to dry. Distress wood, if desired (above). Sand lightly to remove any loose slivers or paint chips and to degloss surface; wipe with tack cloth to remove grit.

2 Apply generous amount of latex or acrylic paint to surface, using a dampened rag; work on one section at a time, applying paint and completing step 3 before moving on to next section.

HOW TO DUPLICATE A CRACKLED PAINT FINISH

MATERIALS

- Crackle medium, such as Quik-Crackle™ by Duncan, available at craft stores.
- Latex or acrylic paint, clear acrylic finish, or aerosol clear acrylic sealer, for base coat.
- Latex or acrylic paint, for crackled coat.
- Sandpaper; tack cloth; sponge applicator or paintbrush.
- Beeswax, clear acrylic finish, or aerosol clear acrylic sealer, for final coat.

1 Prepare the surface as in step 1 for a worn finish, opposite. Apply base coat of paint, clear finish, or aerosol acrylic sealer; if a clear finish or sealer is used, the crackling will reveal the paint or wood color under clear finish. Allow to dry.

2 Apply even, light coat of crackle medium over the base coat; because the crackle medium may tend to run, apply it horizontally whenever possible. Allow to set for length of time specified by the manufacturer or according to your own test results for the desired crackling effect. For a large project, work on a limited area at a time, so you do not exceed setting time.

3 Apply paint in a contrasting color. The paint will start to crackle soon after it is applied; the crackling effect may vary, depending on how heavily the paint is applied over the crackle medium. Allow to dry. Apply beeswax or clear acrylic finish as in step 4 for worn finish, below.

3 Remove some of the paint by rubbing surface with dampened rag, especially in areas that are normally subjected to wear, such as edges and corners. Allow paint to dry completely before moving on to next section.

4 Repeat steps 2 and 3 for the remaining sections. Apply light coat of beeswax over surface, buffing with soft cloth, for subtle sheen. For more durability, clear acrylic finish or several coats of aerosol clear acrylic sealer may be used instead of beeswax.

HOW TO DUPLICATE A CRACKLED & WORN FINISH

MATERIALS

- Materials listed on page 25 for crackled finish; one or more colors of paint may be used for crackled coats.
- Cellulose sponge; clean, lint-free rag.

- Beeswax, clear acrylic finish, or aerosol clear acrylic sealer.

1 Follow steps 1 and 2 for crackled finish on page 25. Apply paint in contrasting color over crackle medium as on page 25, step 3; while paint is still wet, gently wipe over surface in some areas, to remove some of the paint, leaving a thin layer. For a more worn look, rub firmly with a sponge, removing paint down to previous layer. Rinse sponge as necessary.

2 Create additional layers of crackling, if desired, by applying the crackle medium over previous paint after it is dry, to limited areas; then apply the next paint color over those areas. Wipe with a dampened sponge as desired, especially at edges of second paint color. Allow paint to dry. Apply beeswax or clear acrylic finish as in step 4 for worn finish on page 25.

HOW TO DUPLICATE A WEATHERED FINISH

MATERIALS

- Latex or acrylic paint; paintbrush.
- Sandpaper; tack cloth; natural sea sponge.

- Beeswax, clear acrylic finish, or aerosol clear acrylic sealer.

1 Prepare the surface as in step 1 for worn finish on page 24. If the surface is distressed, the completed paint finish will be heavier in the distressed areas.

2 Apply paint, using a paintbrush; work in a small area at a time if the item is large. Allow paint to dry partially; remove some of the paint by holding item under running water from a faucet or garden hose. If paint is too dry to wash away easily, rub surface as necessary.

3 Repeat step 2 for any remaining sections of the item. If too much paint has been removed from some portions, apply additional paint with a dampened sea sponge. Allow item to dry overnight. Apply beeswax or clear acrylic finish as in step 4 for worn finish on page 25.

HOW TO DUPLICATE A SCRUBBED FINISH

MATERIALS

- Item of weathered wood, with some paint remaining on surface.
- Wire brush; coarse-grit sandpaper; tack cloth.
- Paint stripper; putty knife.
- Beeswax.

1 Scrub surface of naturally weathered wood to remove any remaining paint, using wire brush or coarse-grit sandpaper. If paint is difficult to remove, use a paint stripper according to manufacturer's directions. Leave surface in rugged condition; do not sand smooth. Wipe with tack cloth.

2 Rinse the wood thoroughly to remove any remaining residue; allow to dry overnight. Apply a light coat of beeswax over surface, buffing with a soft cloth for a subtle sheen.

HOW TO DUPLICATE A RUSTED OR VERDIGRIS FINISH

MATERIALS

- Primer recommended for type of surface; for a metal surface, use a rust-inhibiting latex metal primer.
- Latex or acrylic paint in black, for base coat.
- Latex or acrylic paint in burnt sienna, for rust finish; latex or acrylic paint in aqua, for verdigris finish.
- Sandpaper; tack cloth; paintbrush; natural sea sponge.

1 Clean the surface to remove any grease and dirt. Rinse with clear water; allow to dry. Sand lightly to degloss the surface; wipe with a tack cloth to remove grit. Apply primer; allow to dry.

2 Apply base coat of black paint. Dip small sea sponge into burnt sienna or aqua paint; blot on a paper towel. Apply to the surface in an up-and-down motion, to give a stippled look. Allow to dry.

GOLD-LEAF FINISH
WITH AN AGED LOOK

A gold-leaf finish with an aged look gives found objects with intricate carved or raised detailing a rich, Old World effect. With its timeless, mellow look, this finish is often used for the picture frames of fine artwork found in museums. Because it may be used on wood, plaster, or cast-resin furnishings, it is also suitable for sconces, candlesticks, and small pieces of furniture. Although the finish requires several steps, the process is easy and the results are exquisite.

For this finish, use imitation gold leaf, sold in craft and art stores. For the dimensional effect, various materials are used in addition to the gold leaf, creating layers and depth. First, a base coat of paint is applied. Then the gold leaf is applied, followed by a clear acrylic sealer that protects the gold leaf from tarnishing. Because the gold leaf is almost translucent, the color of the base coat contributes to the color of the gold leaf. A red base coat, for example, gives a warm, rich gold finish while a white or gold base coat results in a lighter, brighter finish.

The remaining steps are designed to give the worn, Old World look to the finish. A heavy coat of latex or acrylic paint in taupe or cream is applied, then wiped away before it dries, except in the crevices and recessed areas. This is followed by a dusting of rottenstone powder, available at hardware stores, to add texture and aging to the gold-leaf finish.

MATERIALS

- Imitation gold leaf; water-based gold-leaf adhesive.
- Latex or acrylic paint in red or gold, for the base coat.
- Latex or acrylic paint in taupe, beige, or cream, for the top coat.
- Polyvinyl acrylic primer, if item is plaster.
- Rottenstone powder.
- Aerosol clear acrylic sealer.
- Paintbrushes, for applying paint, gold-leaf adhesive, and rottenstone powder; clean, lint-free rags; terry-cloth towel.

Gold-leaf finish may vary, depending on the paint colors used in the process, as you can see in these close-up details. The sconce (near right) has a red base coat under the gold leaf, with a beige top coat. The frame (far right) has a base coat of gold paint under the gold leaf, with a cream top coat.

HOW TO APPLY A GOLD-LEAF FINISH WITH AN AGED LOOK

1 Clean the found object as necessary. Apply a base coat of red or gold paint; allow to dry. If the item is plaster, apply a polyvinyl acrylic primer before applying the base coat.

2 Apply an even, light coat of gold-leaf adhesive, using paintbrush. Allow to set until clear, about one hour; surface will be tacky, but not wet.

3 Cut sheet of imitation gold leaf into smaller, manageable pieces, using scissors. Hold the gold leaf between the supplied tissues; avoid touching it directly with your hands. Slide the bottom tissue from underneath the gold leaf. Touching the top tissue, press gold leaf in place over the adhesive.

4 Remove top tissue. Using soft, dry paintbrush in an up-and-down motion, gently tamp the gold leaf in place to affix it. Then smooth gold leaf, using brush strokes.

5 Continue to apply additional pieces of the gold leaf, overlapping them slightly; the excess gold leaf at the edges will brush away.

6 Fill in any gaps between sheets of gold leaf as desired by applying adhesive and scraps of gold leaf. Apply two coats of aerosol clear acrylic sealer; allow to dry.

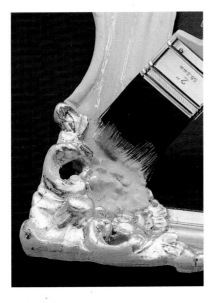

7 Apply a heavy coat of latex or acrylic paint in a burnt umber, taupe, beige, or cream, over the gold leafing. On large project, work on one section at a time, applying the paint and completing step 8 before moving on to the next section.

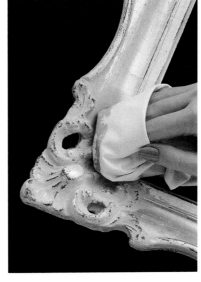

8 Allow paint to partially dry; when paint begins to set, wipe paint off with a clean, lint-free rag. Start by applying light pressure, and then rubbing harder, if necessary. Remove most of the paint in the smooth areas, leaving paint in the carved areas, the crevices, and corners. If paint is difficult to remove, a slightly damp rag may be used.

9 Sprinkle a generous amount of rottenstone powder over the entire project while paint is still slightly damp. Tamp the powder down, using a paintbrush.

10 Leave rottenstone powder on project for 20 minutes; then remove the excess powder with a soft-bristle paintbrush.

11 Buff the raised areas and edges very hard, using terry-cloth towel. Base coat should show in some areas, for a worn effect.

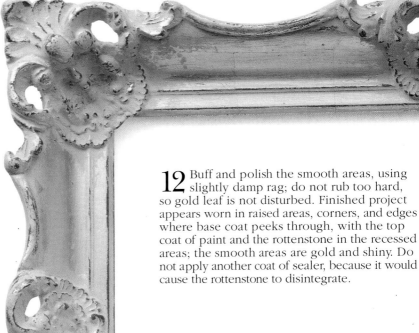

12 Buff and polish the smooth areas, using slightly damp rag; do not rub too hard, so gold leaf is not disturbed. Finished project appears worn in raised areas, corners, and edges where base coat peeks through, with the top coat of paint and the rottenstone in the recessed areas; the smooth areas are gold and shiny. Do not apply another coat of sealer, because it would cause the rottenstone to disintegrate.

REFURBISHING STAINED GLASS PANELS

A stained glass panel makes a dramatic room accent. To show off the reflective quality of the stained glass, hang the panel in a window. Stained glass panels, removed from old houses, churches, and commercial buildings prior to demolition, are available at antique stores, thrift stores, and salvage yards. When selecting a stained glass panel, avoid those that are beginning to cave in, because they can easily collapse. If you find a stained glass panel that needs a replacement part, it can be repaired by a stained glass or leaded glass dealer.

Used stained glass panels will require cleaning and polishing. In addition to shining the stained glass, you may want to refinish or paint the wood frame. To display the panel, hangers may be secured to the frame.

HOW TO HANG A STAINED GLASS PANEL

Secure hooks to the top of the stained glass panel frame and to the top of the window frame, predrilling the holes. Hang the panel from chains secured to the hooks. Use chains and hooks that are strong enough to support the weight of the panel, keeping in mind that the weight is distributed between the two sets of chains and hooks.

TIPS FOR REFURBISHING STAINED GLASS PANELS

Remove old paint from stained glass by applying mineral spirits to the area covered with paint, using a paintbrush; wait a moment, and scrape away paint with a razor blade. Or remove putty or glazing compound from the glass, using vinegar and a razor blade; do not use a heat gun, because it may crack the glass or melt the lead.

Clean dirty lead by rubbing 0000 steel wool over it, taking care not to scratch the glass; then wipe the lead with a dampened cloth.

Clean glass, using a commercial-grade cleaner, if available; or use a standard glass cleaner.

Polish glass, using a commercial polish or a finishing compound; wipe the polish on, allow it to dry, and buff the surface. Or use furniture polish to shine the glass. Polish gives the glass a protective wax coating.

RENOVATING OLD TRUNKS

Before *these dirty trunks were renovated, they had dull finishes, worn linings, and broken hardware and straps.*

Old trunks, chests, and footlockers can be cleaned and refurbished to become functional and decorative accent pieces. Use them as alternatives to coffee tables and end tables or as display cases brimming with antique dolls, teddy bears, or old quilts. To retain the authentic look of aging, simply clean the trunk and enjoy its worn appearance. Or make a few simple repairs on the trunk, such as patching torn tin or replacing broken hardware with reproduction pieces.

solution, such as vinegar and water or Murphy's Oil Soap™ and water. Allow the trunk to dry thoroughly, preferably outdoors in direct sunlight. If the odor still persists, clean the trunk again, using a diluted bleach solution. When dry, seal the inside with a clear acrylic finish. It may not always be possible to completely remove the odor from the wood; in that case, you may want to place cedar blocks or chips inside the completed trunk as a freshener.

CLEANING TRUNKS

In general, when cleaning trunks, start with the gentlest method, and increase the harshness of the cleaning process as necessary. When cleaning wood, start with denatured alcohol; this provides gentle cleaning and often renews the color of the wood.

Because old trunks are often stored in basements and cellars, they may have a musty odor. There are steps that can be taken to remove this odor. Strip any lining paper or fabric by moistening and scraping it. Next, clean the inside of the trunk thoroughly, using a mild cleaning

TRUNK CONSTRUCTION & HARDWARE

Old trunks generally have a wooden framework covered with tin, canvas, leather, or cabinet wood. Several wooden staves may be attached to the sides and top of the trunk to protect the surface. These staves are secured with clamps.

Most trunks feature large center locks with drawbolts positioned on both sides of the lock to guide the lid to fit the bottom section. Most locks and drawbolts can be replaced, if necessary. Specialty mail-order suppliers offer an extensive variety of reproduction hardware pieces for old trunks. Select replacement hardware in a similar size

After *renovation, the trunks are renewed with polishing and painting, and broken straps and old linings are replaced.*

and style. Be sure to determine whether the center lock is a set-in or surface lock. Hardware was usually secured to trunks with nails that were longer than the thickness of the wood; the ends of the nails were "curled" on the inside, or turned back into the wood, for a secure mount. Replacement parts should be installed using the same method, as on page 37. Missing leather handles and straps can often be replaced with sections of belts, and shoe repair shops can provide repair services for leather.

LINING TRUNKS

Many trunks were lined with paper and will need relining. For an authentic look, choose a wallcovering in a color and pattern that is appropriate for the age of the trunk. Small prints and narrow stripes work well.

Some trunks had elaborate designs on the inside of the lid. When stripping the original paper, preserve these designs whenever possible by cutting around the design with a razor knife. Complete all cleaning and any exterior repairs on the trunk before replacing the old lining with wallcovering.

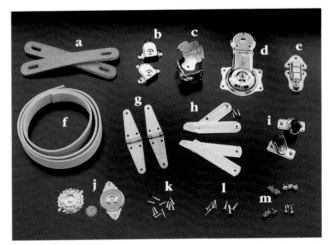

Replacement parts for trunks include: leather handles **(a)**, trunk loops **(b)** for securing leather handles, clamps and corner pieces **(c)**, locks **(d)**, drawbolts **(e)**, leather straps and loops **(f)**, hinges **(g)**, side stays or support hinges **(h)**, casters **(i)**, and brass ornaments **(j)**. Trunk nails **(k)** and split rivets **(l)** are available in several lengths, and decorative nails **(m)** are available in many styles.

TIPS FOR CLEANING TRUNKS

Cleaning leather.
Use rag and saddle soap to clean the leather; allow to dry. Then polish the leather, and replenish oil with leather dressing, such as mink oil. Use all-purpose cement to reglue any tears.

Cleaning canvas.
Scrub the canvas gently, using a brush and mild cleanser. Reglue any loose areas, using wood glue diluted with an equal amount of water.

Cleaning tin. Use rag and a solution of equal parts of vinegar and water to clean tin. Remove any rust (right).

Cleaning casters. Scrub the casters, using wire brush and hot, soapy water. Allow to dry; then lubricate with aerosol silicone.

Removing rust. Use fine steel wool and lubricant oil to remove rust; wipe with mineral spirits to remove the oil residue.

TIPS FOR REPAIRING TIN

Repairing holes or tears. Use Liquid Steel® filler to patch any holes or tears in the tin; sand smooth. Touch up with primer and paint (right).

Replacing damaged area. Cut away old tin, using tin snips, and nail on new pieces; use smooth tin from sheet-metal shops or embossed tin from specialty suppliers. Use Liquid Steel filler to bridge the ridge between old tin and the replacement section. Touch up with primer, and paint (right).

Painting tin. Use masking tape to protect the surrounding area. Apply a rust-inhibiting metal primer; then apply rust-inhibiting enamel paint.

HOW TO REPLACE A CURVED WOOD STAVE

1 Soak slat of birch, hickory, or other bendable wood for several days, until saturated; weight down to keep slat immersed.

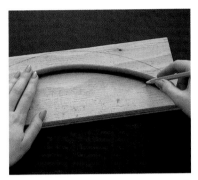

2 Shape a flexible curve to match the curve of the trunk. Mark the curve on sheet of ¾" (2 cm) plywood. Draw a second marked line about 1" (2.5 cm) below the first line as shown; mark the ends to complete pattern for the jig.

3 Glue two sheets of ¾" (2 cm) plywood together. Place the marked plywood on top; glue and screw layers together, inserting screws outside marked lines. Allow to dry; cut on marked lines.

4 Glue and screw the curved piece to a base piece of plywood; allow jig to dry. Clamp to table.

5 Clamp slat to outer curved edge of the jig, near one end; to protect the slat, place a scrap of wood under the clamp. Bend slat; clamp 4" to 6" (10 to 15 cm) from the first clamp. Continue to bend and clamp slat along curve of jig at 4" to 6" (10 to 15 cm) intervals. Allow stave to dry thoroughly; finish the wood to match the other staves. Secure to trunk.

TIPS FOR REMOVING & REPLACING NAILS, TACKS & HARDWARE

Removing "curled" nails. Check for curled nail tips before removing any old nails. If tip of nail is turned into wood on inside of trunk, straighten or cut off tip. You may need to dig into the wood slightly, using a tack puller.

Removing nails and tacks. Use a tack puller to remove nails and tacks. Protect surface by placing a shim under tool; this prevents denting surface of the trunk.

Installing "curled" nails. Curl nails when installing hardware by using a nail ¼" (6 mm) longer than thickness of wood and hardware. Place a heavy metal object, such as an old iron, inside the trunk when pounding the nail.

(Continued)

TIPS FOR REMOVING & REPLACING NAILS, TACKS, & HARDWARE
(CONTINUED)

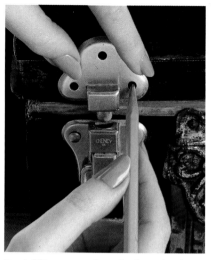

Aging new hardware. Remove the lacquer from hardware to allow natural aging to occur by placing hardware in boiling water; leave it in the boiling water as long as necessary to loosen lacquer. Remove loosened lacquer, using steel wool.

Attaching new hardware. Attach hardware through weakened wood or old nail holes, using a split rivet that is at least ¼" (6 mm) longer than the thickness of wood and hardware, and place a washer on the inside of trunk. Flatten ends of rivet against washer.

Installing new drawbolt or lock. Replace bottom section of drawbolt or lock. Then lower the lid and close the drawbolt or lock; align the top section, and mark placement for nails. Secure one nail, and recheck fit; then secure remaining nails.

HOW TO LINE A TRUNK WITH WALLCOVERING

MATERIALS

- Wallcovering.
- Wallcovering adhesive and seam adhesive, if necessary.
- Decorative trim, such as ribbon or gimp.

- Sponge; razor knife; seam roller or brayer; putty knife.
- Aerosol clear acrylic sealer; sandpaper; tack cloth; craft glue.

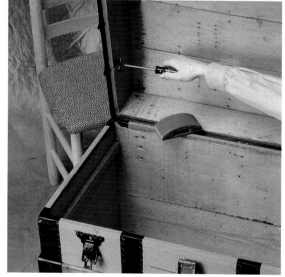

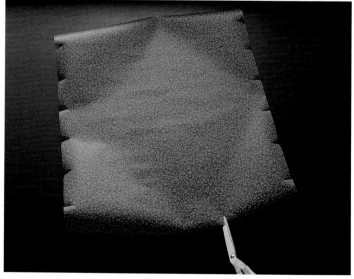

1 Apply aerosol clear acrylic sealer to the interior; sand lightly, to degloss surface. Wipe with tack cloth. Remove side stay from trunk; brace lid with chair or other support to avoid damaging hinges.

2 Measure one side of the trunk base; cut wallcovering 2" (5 cm) wider and 5" (25.5 cm) longer than measurements. Repeat for the opposite side. Cut 1" (2.5 cm) slits in wallcovering pieces on sides and lower edges, at 3" to 4" (7.5 to 10 cm) intervals.

3 Prepare prepasted wallcovering or apply wallcovering adhesive, according to the manufacturer's instructions. Press the wallcovering into place on sides of trunk base, extending the clipped edges onto back, front, and bottom of trunk; smooth wallcovering in place around any tray supports. Smooth out any bubbles or wrinkles, using a dampened sponge.

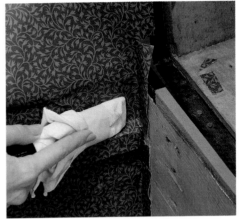

4 Trim and notch wallcovering at ends of tray supports. Press wallcovering into place, using a putty knife wrapped with a clean rag or paper towel.

5 Trim the excess wallcovering even with the upper edge of trunk base, using a razor knife. If wallcovering does not adhere well along upper edges, apply a bead of seam adhesive.

6 Measure back, bottom, and front as one unit; cut wallcovering to this measurement plus 2" (5 cm). Apply wallcovering, smoothing it from center bottom of trunk upward onto the back of trunk, then onto the front. Trim excess even with upper edge, using razor knife. Apply additional widths of wallcovering as necessary.

7 Line trunk lid, as in steps 2 to 6. Glue reproduction lid design to center of lid, if desired; or, if trunk has original lid design, cut hole in wallcovering to expose design, using razor knife.

8 Glue gimp trim or ribbon to upper edge of trunk base, if desired, using thick craft glue and butting the ends in one corner; repeat for the lid top. Outline the lid design with gimp or ribbon, if desired.

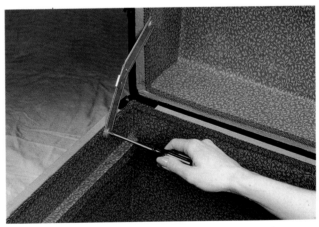

9 Secure upper half of side stay to lid, using wood screw; open the side stay. With lid upright and at a 90° angle to the base, mark screw location for lower half of stay. Secure, using wood screw.

Armoires not only provide needed storage, but also make wonderful display cases for collectibles, such as china and crystal, toys, books, and quilts. Provide a decorative backdrop to the display by lining the armoire with fabric or wallcovering. If you plan to keep the doors of the armoire open, you may want to reverse them to show off decorative door fronts.

To line an armoire with fabric, without using damaging adhesives or staples, wrap heavy cardboard with the fabric and apply it to the inside of the armoire with pieces of self-adhesive hook and loop tape. A thin layer of polyester fleece, placed between the cardboard and the fabric, adds a light padding.

Before lining an armoire with wallcovering, lightly sand the wood in order to degloss the finish and ensure good adhesion. Most wallcoverings will adhere without applying a wallcovering primer. If a primer is used, returning the armoire to its original finish at some future date would be more difficult.

Armoires *may be lined with wallcovering (opposite) or fabric (below) to neatly finish off the interior.*

MATERIALS

- Mediumweight, firmly woven fabric.
- Polyester fleece.
- Self-adhesive hook and loop tape.
- Heavy cardboard, or foam-core board.
- Aerosol adhesive intended for use with fabric.
- Fabric glue.
- Mat knife.

1 Remove any shelves and shelf supports from armoire.

2 Cut the cardboard ¼" (6 mm) smaller than the length and width of the armoire back, using a mat knife and straightedge. Check fit of cardboard in armoire.

3 Cut polyester fleece slightly larger than the cardboard. Apply aerosol adhesive to one side of cardboard; affix fleece to cardboard. Trim the edges of fleece even with edges of cardboard.

4 Cut fabric 4" (10 cm) larger than cardboard. Center the cardboard, fleece side down, on the wrong side of fabric. Wrap fabric around cardboard at the corners and sides as shown; glue in place.

5 Cut short strips of self-adhesive hook and loop tape. Press the hook side and loop side of tape together; affix to back of the armoire, at the corners and at intervals as desired.

6 Position covered cardboard on armoire back; press into place, pressing against hook and loop tape strips, to affix cardboard to armoire. Repeat steps 2 to 5 for sides of armoire without shelves; position in armoire.

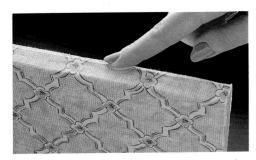

7 Cover the shelves, if any, using rectangle of fabric cut to fit length of shelf; wrap the fabric around shelf, securing overlapped fabric on the back edge. Secure raw edges of fabric, using glue diluted with water.

8 Reinstall the shelf supports and the shelves. Cover sides of the armoire with shelves by cutting cardboard ¼" (6 mm) smaller than the length and width of each section between shelves. Cover the cardboard and install as in steps 3 to 6. This method may also be used to cover the bottom of armoire and any framed insets.

HOW TO LINE AN ARMOIRE WITH WALLCOVERING

MATERIALS

- Wallcovering; wallcovering adhesive, if necessary.
- Aerosol clear acrylic sealer; sandpaper; tack cloth.
- Smoothing brush; seam roller or brayer.
- Razor knife; straightedge.

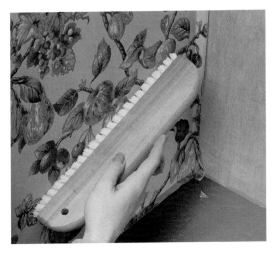

1 Remove shelves and shelf supports. Apply aerosol clear acrylic sealer to interior; sand lightly to degloss the surface. Wipe with tack cloth. Cut wallcovering strip 1" (2.5 cm) wider and longer than side of the armoire. Moisten the prepasted wallcovering, or apply wallcovering adhesive. Position the wallcovering, and then smooth in place; extend onto back and bottom for ½" (1.3 cm), clipping as necessary.

2 Trim the wallcovering at the upper and front edges, using a straightedge and a razor knife.

3 Cut the wallcovering strip or strips 1" (2.5 cm) longer than back of armoire; apply the first strip to back, lapping over extension at side of armoire. Trim upper edge.

4 Apply additional strip or strips to the back of armoire, trimming last strip to extend ½" (1.3 cm) onto the side. Cut and apply wallcovering to the remaining side, lapping over back extension and trimming upper and front edges.

5 Cut wallcovering to fit bottom; apply. Cover the shelves with wallcovering as in step 7, above, applying the adhesive to entire piece. Locate the holes for shelf support hardware; reinstall shelf supports and shelves.

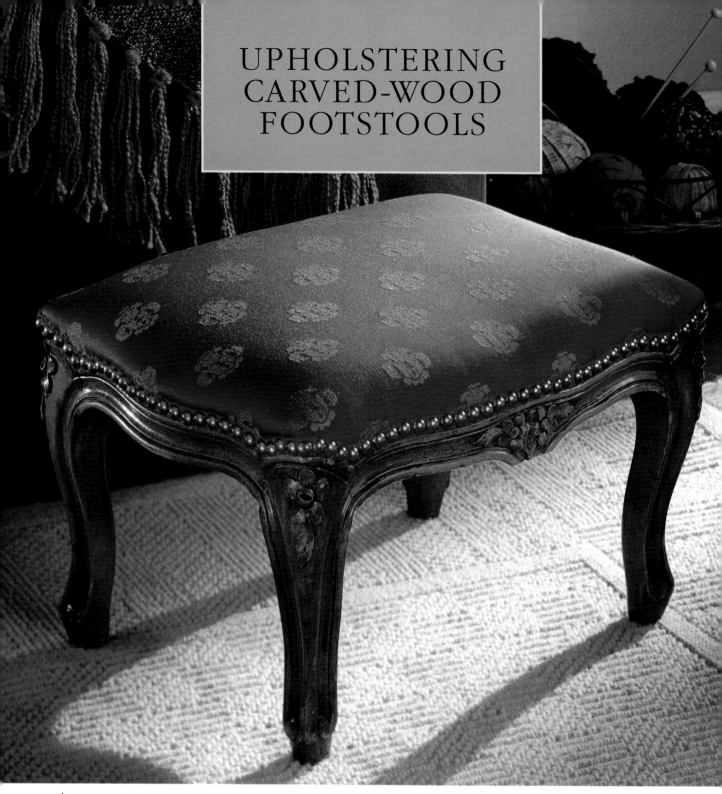

UPHOLSTERING CARVED-WOOD FOOTSTOOLS

Among the great finds at antique stores are footstools with lovely carved wood. If the wood frame is still in good condition, the footstool can be restored to like-new by replacing the upholstery. Covered with a traditional fabric, such as tapestry or hand-stitched needlepoint, and trimmed with contrasting gimp or decorative nails, the footstool becomes a handsome room accessory.

Sometimes you will find more than one layer of fabric on the footstool, if a previous owner recovered it without removing the old fabric. Before you upholster it, strip all layers of old fabric from the stool, removing the tacks

or decorative nails with an upholstery hammer and a screwdriver. This allows you to replace the old padding, for more comfort and a smoother, softer appearance.

In most cases, if the footstool has springs, the twines that once held them in place are broken. For the easiest method of upholstery, remove the springs, eliminating the need for retying them. Also remove the webbing, which has usually sagged and deteriorated, and replace it with new webbing on the top of the frame. Before you begin upholstering, you may want to refinish the wood frame.

HOW TO UPHOLSTER A FOOTSTOOL

MATERIALS

- Decorator fabric, such as tapestry fabric, or hand-stitched needlepoint.
- Jute upholstery webbing, 4" (10 cm) wide.
- Polyurethane foam in 1" (2.5 cm) thickness; aerosol foam adhesive.
- Polyester or cotton upholstery batting.
- Burlap, for support under the foam.
- Cambric or muslin, for dustcover on bottom of footstool.

- Gimp trim; use gimp that matches fabric if decorative upholstery nails are being applied over the gimp, or use matching or contrasting color if gimp is used alone as a decorative edging.
- Decorative upholstery nails, optional; small-headed upholstery hammer for inserting decorative nails.
- Heavy-duty stapler (electric stapler is recommended) and ½" (1.3 cm) staples.
- Hot glue gun and glue sticks.

1 Remove all layers of old fabric from the stool, removing decorative nails and tacks with a small hammer and a screwdriver. Then remove the old padding, webbing, and springs, if any.

2 Determine the number of webbing strips that can be applied in each direction; the strips should not be spaced more than 1" (2.5 cm) apart. Mark placement of strips on the upper edge of the frame, using pencil. Cut webbing strips 4" (10 cm) longer than the frame.

3 Secure one strip of webbing to upper edge of the frame; fold up ½" (1.3 cm) at end of webbing, and staple through both layers, using five staples. On the opposite side of frame, staple the webbing to frame through a single layer, pulling the webbing tight with pliers.

4 Fold up end of the webbing strip, and staple again through both layers. Trim end of the webbing to ½" (1.3 cm).

5 Repeat for remaining parallel strips. Secure webbing strips to frame in opposite direction, weaving them over and under the previous strips. Staple all strips as in steps 3 and 4, stretching them tight with pliers.

6 Cut burlap 3" (7.5 cm) larger than the footstool frame. Fold under edge of burlap piece; staple it to the top of frame, over the webbing, at 1½" (3.8 cm) intervals, stretching burlap taut.

(Continued)

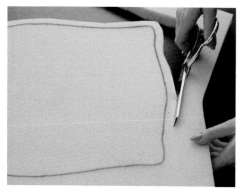

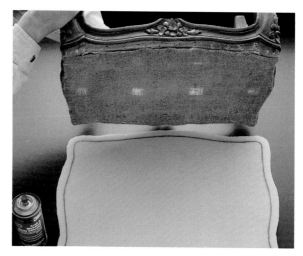

7 Place footstool upside down on foam; draw outline of frame on foam, using pencil. Cut foam ½" (1.3 cm) beyond the marked lines, using scissors.

8 Apply aerosol adhesive to marked side of foam and to the burlap. Place the footstool upside down on foam, pressing down so foam adheres to the burlap. Stand footstool right side up; press down on foam.

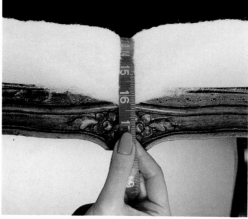

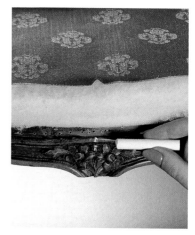

9 Place a layer of upholstery batting over foam, wrapping it around the sides of footstool; trim excess batting above the decorative wood.

10 Measure footstool length and width from decorative wood on one side, over foam and batting, to decorative wood on opposite side. Add 5" (12.5 cm) to these measurements; cut decorator fabric to this size.

11 Notch center of each side of fabric; mark decorative wood on center of each side of footstool frame, using chalk.

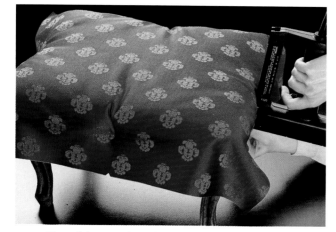

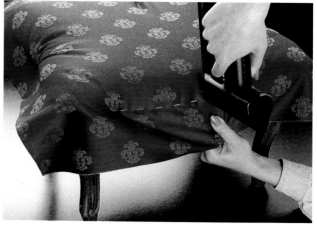

12 Place fabric, right side up, over batting. Staple-baste center of fabric at center on front of frame, just above decorative wood, then at center on back of frame, stretching fabric slightly. Repeat in other direction, staple-basting fabric at center of each side; this centers fabric on frame.

13 Remove the center staple from front of frame; stretch fabric taut, and staple again at center. Working from center toward one side, apply staples at 1" (2.5 cm) intervals, stretching fabric taut; stop 3" (7.5 cm) from corner. Repeat, working from center toward opposite side.

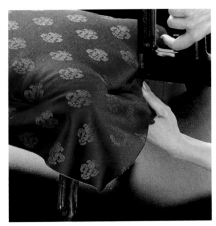

14 Repeat step 13 on back of the footstool, stretching fabric taut; then repeat for sides of stool.

15 Stretch fabric at corner, dividing the excess fullness equally on each side of corner; insert one staple, centered above the leg, just above decorative wood.

16 Fold fabric as shown, forming an inverted pleat, or "V," at the corner, folding out all excess fabric. Staple in place. Repeat at remaining corners.

18 Glue gimp above the decorative wood, using hot glue gun, starting at center of one side; make sure that the raw edges and staples are covered. Fold under ½" (1.3 cm) at ends of gimp, and butt folded ends together. Omit step 19 if decorative nails are not being used.

17 Finish stapling each side at 1" (2.5 cm) intervals, up to corners, stretching the fabric taut. Trim excess fabric on all sides of footstool, just above decorative wood.

19 Tap the decorative nails into wood, using upholstery hammer; center nails over gimp. Check position of each nail before pounding in; if necessary, adjust vertical or horizontal position by tapping side of nail head slightly. Insert the nails head-to-head all around footstool; if any nail heads are damaged, replace nail with a new one.

20 Cut cambric or muslin 2" (5 cm) larger than bottom of footstool. Fold under the edges of cambric or muslin; staple to the bottom of the footstool at 1" (2.5 cm) intervals.

MIRRORS FROM OLD WINDOWS

For a creative accessory, turn an old window into a wall mirror, providing an element of surprise in your home decorating.

To make a mirror from an old window, simply remove the glass, replacing it with mirrors that are cut to fit within the window openings. On most window frames, the glass is secured with glazing and glazing points that need to be removed. The easiest way to remove the glazing is by softening it with a heat gun and scraping it off with a putty knife. An inexpensive heat gun will work well for this purpose; heat guns may also be rented. The mirror can then be held in place with glazing points only.

Cabinet doors with windows are usually assembled with a narrow wood beading that holds the glass in place. The beading can easily be removed by prying it off; it can then be replaced after the mirror is inserted.

Old windows are easy to find at salvage yards, antique stores,

Old windows are converted into wall mirrors by replacing the glass with custom-cut pieces of mirror. The window shown above has a stained finish; a single mirror pane is secured using the window's wood beading. Opposite, a weathered window has several small panes, held in place with glazing points.

and thrift stores, at affordable prices. Select one that has a sturdy frame, to ensure that it will support the mirror securely.

Window frames with mullions are especially attractive when used for mirrors. On some windows, each mullion frames a separate pane of glass; for these windows, a separate mirror must be cut to fit within each opening. Other window frames with mullions have a single opening with one large sheet of glass set into it, and the mullions are simply used as a decorative trim placed in front of the glass.

Mirrors may be ordered in custom sizes at glass supply stores and specialty mirror stores. Remove the old glazing and glass before ordering the mirrors, so you can accurately measure the openings of the window frame. Measure each opening individually to check for any variance in the sizes. Record the measurements for each opening on a sketch of the window.

MATERIALS

- Old window.
- Mirror of ⅛" (3 mm) thickness, cut to fit within rabbet, or recess, of each opening.
- Mat board, for backing.
- Glazing points, if old window has glazing.

- Two swivel hangers and screws, to mount onto back of mirror frame; two picture hangers or mirror hangers, to mount onto wall. Select hangers that will support the weight of the mirror.
- Heat gun; putty knife.

HOW TO MAKE A MIRROR FROM AN OLD WINDOW

1 Window with glazing and glazing points. Soften the glazing around the edges of glass panes, using a heat gun on a high setting; hold the heat gun 4" (10 cm) from glazing, until the surface is heated. Stop heating if the paint begins to bubble.

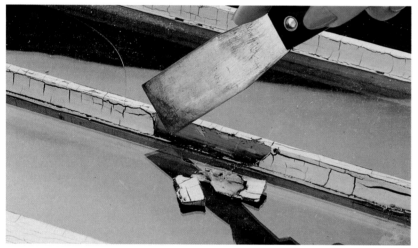

2 Scrape glazing with a putty knife to remove it. If necessary, repeat the process of softening and scraping the glazing. Take care to remove the glazing from corners of opening.

3 Pry out the metal glazing points that are set into the wood next to the glass, using screwdriver. Allow glass to cool.

4 Remove glass panes. Scrape off any remaining glazing from wood moldings. Clean the window frame and preserve the finish (pages 18 to 21). Or apply a finish with an aged look, if desired (pages 22 to 27).

5 Insert the mirrors, facedown, into the openings. Cut mat board to same sizes as openings; place on top of mirrors. Mat boards prevent the silver on back of mirror from becoming scratched.

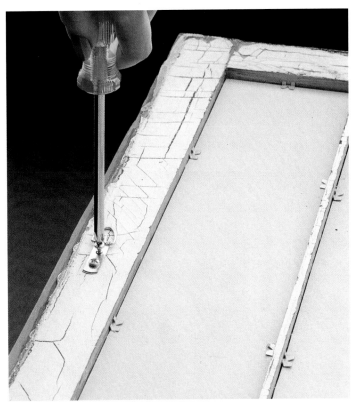

6 Insert glazing points into window frame on all sides of opening, pushing them into place with a putty knife.

7 Mark the placement for the swivel hangers on sides of frame, about one-third of the way down from the top; predrill the holes for the screws. Secure swivel hangers with screws.

8 Measure and mark placement for mirror or picture hangers on wall, equal to distance between swivel hangers on frame; use a carpenter's level to ensure that the marks are level. Secure mirror or picture hangers at markings. Hang mirror.

Window with wood beading. Pry off the wood beading, using screwdriver; remove the glass. Insert mirror and mat board as in step 5, opposite. Replace beading. Hang mirror as in steps 7 and 8.

POT RACKS FROM OLD WINDOWS

A pot rack can be made from an old window hung from the ceiling with strong hooks and chains. Select a sturdy window frame in good condition, and strengthen the corner joints with corner braces. To support the weight of the window frame and heavy pots, use the hardware items below, which support about 30 lb. (13.5 kg) each. Because the weight is supported at four locations, the total weight of the frame and the pots can be up to 120 lb. (54 kg).

MATERIALS

- Old window; corner braces.
- #6 zinc screw eyes and heavy chain, to hang frame.
- #6 zinc ceiling hooks, to hang pots.
- Swag hooks, to hang chains from ceiling.

HOW TO MAKE A POT RACK FROM AN OLD WINDOW

1 Remove the glazing and glass from the window frame (page 52). Clean the frame thoroughly, scraping off any loose paint; apply a fresh coat of paint or a clear acrylic finish.

2 Reinforce frame on top side with corner braces. Predrill holes and insert screw eyes near corners. Open one link of the chain, inserting screw eye; reclose link.

3 Predrill holes and insert ceiling hooks **(a)** on underside of frame. Secure swag hooks **(b)** into ceiling joists if possible, or use toggle bolts. Hang chains from swag hooks.

MORE IDEAS FOR OLD WINDOWS

Honeysuckle and silk ivy (above) encircle this crackled window frame, for a decorative wall display. To create the effect of a windowsill, a board is added at the bottom.

Scenic print (left) is displayed in the window of a cabinet door, rather than in a picture frame. The print was mounted as for a mirror (pages 51 to 53).

TABLES FROM OLD DOORS

An old solid-wood door can be converted into a table simply by cutting off the ends of the door and using them as table legs. For quick assembly, the legs are secured with corner braces, making a sturdy table. The original finish of the door may be preserved or a new finish may be applied, depending on how rustic you want the table to be.

For matching legs and a symmetrical tabletop, select a paneled door with panels of equal size. The end piece on the bottom of the door is usually wider than the end piece on the top. To make both legs alike, the bottom of the door can be cut off to match the top of the door, as shown in steps 1 and 2.

A sheet of polished glass can be placed on top of the table; custom-cut glass may be ordered from

glass retailers. The glass may be cushioned, using clear acrylic discs or felt self-adhesive bumpers, available from hardware stores.

MATERIALS

- Old solid-wood paneled door.
- Eight 1½" (3.8 cm) double-wide corner braces; 6 × 1" (2.5 cm) wood screws.
- Circular saw or table saw; drill and ⅛" drill bit.

HOW TO MAKE A TABLE FROM AN OLD DOOR

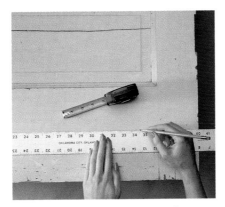
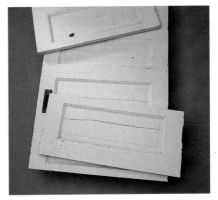

1 Remove hinges and hardware from door, if desired. Clean the door; preserve the finish as on pages 18 to 21, if desired. Measure end piece from top of door to upper door panel.

2 Mark a line on end piece at bottom of door, measuring from lower door panel a distance equal to measurement from step 1. Cut on marked line, using saw; discard end piece.

3 Plan and measure desired height of leg pieces; mark, and cut on the marked lines. Remaining center portion of door is used for tabletop; for a shorter tabletop, cut off and discard one or more of the door panels.

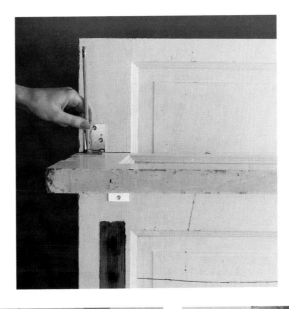

4 Place tabletop section facedown. Set the leg pieces on top, inset about 8" (20.5 cm) from ends of the tabletop. Using pencil, mark the placement of the legs on the tabletop, parallel to ends.

5 Place four 1½" (3.8 cm) double-wide corner braces next to leg, with two braces on each side of leg. Keeping leg aligned with marked line, mark holes for placement of screws; stagger the braces as necessary so screws will not hit each other.

6 Predrill holes for the screws, using ⅛" drill bit; secure braces with 6 × 1" (2.5 cm) wood screws.

7 Sand edges of tabletop; apply the desired finish to edges if the finish of the door was preserved in step 1; the edges may contrast with other surfaces. Entire table may be finished with an aged look, as on pages 22 to 27, or painted.

Several doors are converted into a room divider.

Determine the hinge placement and in which direction the doors will fold; hinges may be removed and turned around, in order to fold in the opposite direction. To join the doors, the existing hinge of one door is attached to the edge of the next door. If the edge is mortised, it may be necessary to enlarge the mortised area with a chisel to accommodate the hinge of the previous door. Fill mortised areas that are too large with wood filler. Sometimes, the existing hinge of one door may be attached flush to the edge of the next door.

Paneled door (above) is placed on four columns to create a desk. Polished glass, custom-cut to size, is placed over the door.

Old door (right) is leaned against the wall as an unusual display piece in a room with an eclectic mix of furnishings.

Bench is made from a long, narrow door as on pages 56 and 57.

SHELVES FROM OLD SHUTTERS

Shutters contribute a casual feeling to a room, while offering interesting texture and color. Old shutters are easily adapted for a variety of new uses, including the decorative corner shelving units shown here and the creative display ideas on pages 62 and 63.

For a wide selection of old shutters, visit a salvage yard that has building materials. If you find painted shutters that have not yet weathered, you may want to apply one of the finishes on pages 22 to 27, for an aged look. If you prefer a stained wood finish in good condition, you may find more suitable shutters at antique stores, but you can expect to pay more for them.

To make corner shelves from shutters, select shutters that are structurally solid and unwarped. Cut the triangular shelves from lumber, and trim the diagonal edges of the shelves with wood moldings.

MATERIALS

- Two shutters of the same size.
- Medium-density fiberboard or plywood in desired thickness, for shelves.
- Shelf molding or panel molding, for edges of shelves.
- ½" × ½" (1.3 × 1.3 cm) cove or inside corner molding, for shelf supports.
- ½" × ¾" (1.3 × 2 cm) parting stop, cut 2" (5 cm) shorter than shutters, to join shutters.
- 17 × 1" (2.5 cm) brads, for attaching moldings.
- Finish nails, for attaching parting stop and shelf supports.
- Wood glue; jigsaw; drill; ¹⁄₁₆" drill bit.

Corner shelves made from old shutters may stand on the floor (left) or hang on the wall (below). To hang the shelving unit, use three sawtooth hangers, one near the corner and two at the outer edges of the shutter frame. Rubber bumpers, placed at the bottom, keep hanging shelves level.

1 Cut one end of panel molding **(a)** or shelf molding **(b)** for shelves at 45° angle, using miter box, with direction of angle as shown. Measure angled edge as indicated; do not measure the rabbet, if using panel molding.

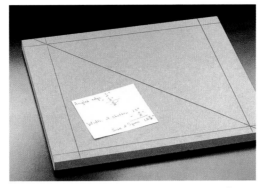

2 Add ⅛" (3 mm) to the measurement from step 1; subtract from width of the shutter. Mark a square this size on lumber for shelves; draw a diagonal line through square. Using a jigsaw, cut lumber on marked lines to make two shelves. Cut any additional shelves.

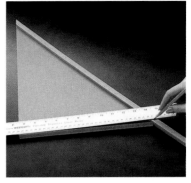

3 Align mitered end of molding to the diagonal edge of shelf; mark finished length and angle of miter cut at the opposite end. For each shelf, cut one molding strip, to be used as edge trim.

4 Cut one strip of cove molding for each shelf support, mitering the ends; length of the support is equal to length of the short side of triangular piece.

5 Apply wood glue to diagonal edge of the shelf; position the molding on edge. Predrill nail holes with 1⁄16" drill bit, at ends and center. Secure molding with brads. Set brads, using nail set.

6 Determine desired placement for shelves; mark the shutters with placement line for bottom of shelf. Mask off frame of shutters below marked line, using ⅜" (1 cm) strip of tape; mask off back edges of shutters.

7 Paint shutters, apply finish with aged look (pages 22 to 27), or preserve finish (pages 18 to 21); do not apply finish to areas that are masked off. Finish shelves, shelf supports, and parting stop to match shutters. Remove tape.

8 Position parting stop on shutter, centering it on length of shutter and aligning front edges. Predrill nail holes through parting stop and into frame, about 1" (2.5 cm) from ends and at 4" (10 cm) intervals. To secure parting stop, sand the edge, glue, and nail. Repeat to secure parting stop to remaining shutter, taking care to avoid previous nails.

9 Sand back edges of the shelf supports. Position supports with upper edge just covering the placement lines; predrill nail holes through support and into frame of shutter. Secure supports to shutters, using glue and nails. Place shelves on supports.

MORE IDEAS
FOR OLD SHUTTERS

Shutter, hung in the kitchen, serves as a rack for cooking utensils, lightweight pots, and copper molds. The items are hung from S-hooks.

Clean the shutter thoroughly, and apply a clear acrylic finish before using it to hang kitchen utensils. Secure the shutter to the wall, using drywall screws. If you are not able to screw into wall studs, use plastic anchors in predrilled holes to support the weight of the shutter.

Massive wall display features shutters instead of artwork. The shutters, given a weathered finish (page 26), are hung with swivel hangers as shown opposite.

Tabletop display (above) includes shutters that form a backdrop for a collection of accessories.

Shutters (right) are hung on the wall next to the window, for a country look. Hang the shutters as shown below.

Attach swivel hangers to the back of the shutter, about one-third down from the top; hang the shutter from picture hangers or mirror hangers.

CANDLESTICKS FROM OLD BALUSTERS

Balusters from staircases are often among the architectural finds in antique stores and salvage yards. These turned, and often quite ornamental, wooden posts are ripped out of old buildings before demolition. Available in various designs, they can easily become candlesticks, provided they are at least 2" (5 cm) in diameter. The balusters need not be in perfect condition. The usual nicks and scratches that come from years of wear add character to the piece. The newel post from the foot or landing of a demolished staircase may also be used for a candlestick.

To make a candlestick, cut a base and an upper platform from a separate piece of wood. If you are planning to maintain a natural or stained wood finish, select the type of wood used for the baluster, whenever possible, and stain the base to match (left). Or you may want to mimic the aged finishes of balusters, such as the weathered finish on page 26 (middle and right).

HOW TO MAKE A CANDLESTICK FROM AN OLD BALUSTER

MATERIALS

- Old baluster, at least 2" (5 cm) in diameter.
- 1 × lumber, to be used for the base and upper platform of candlestick.
- Wood stain or paint in desired color or colors, optional.
- Wood glue.
- 5d nail, 1½" (3.8 cm) long, to hold candle in place.
- Backsaw; clamps; drill and 1/16" drill bit.

1 Clean the old baluster with mild soapy water; allow to dry. Saw post to desired height, using a backsaw.

2 Cut two square pieces from 1 × board for base of the candlestick, with one piece 1" (2.5 cm) and one 3" (7.5 cm) larger than diameter of post at bottom.

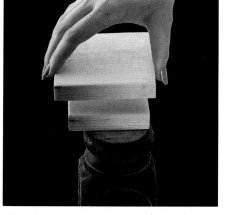

3 Cut two square pieces from the 1 × lumber for upper platform, with one piece ¾" (2 cm) larger and one 1½" (3.8 cm) larger than diameter of post at top.

4 Apply desired stain or paint finish to the post and squares of lumber.

5 Drill through center of larger piece for upper platform, using 1/16" drill bit. From bottom of piece, hammer nail into center hole; nail will protrude from top of piece, to be used for holding the candle in place.

6 Apply wood glue to the bottom of piece with nail; clamp to smaller piece for the upper platform. Apply wood glue to the bottom of smaller base piece; clamp to the larger base piece. Allow glue to dry.

7 Apply small amount of wood glue to bottom and top of post. Center base on bottom of post, with smaller section of base next to post. Center the upper platform on post, with smaller section of platform next to post. Clamp until glue dries.

MORE IDEAS FOR ARCHITECTURAL FINDS

Balcony rail (*left*) *serves as the base for a table.*

Screw the brackets of the balcony rail directly to the wall, and paint the screw heads to match the rail. If the brackets cannot be located at wall studs, use molly bolts.

Old mantel (*below*) *becomes a ledge for propped-up pictures. Two of the pictures are overlapped for added interest.*

Attach swivel hangers to the back of mantel; attach rubber bumpers near the bottom, below swivel hangers, to keep the mantel level when hung on the wall.

Vintage fireplace surround *substitutes for a working fireplace. An antique fireplace screen, placed in front of the opening, increases the realistic effect.*

Aged pilasters *(right) from an outdoor entry flank a small cabinet.*

Nail the pilasters into the wall studs, inserting the nails through the side boards; angle the nails downward for added strength. Set the nails, using a nail set.

WINDOW TREATMENTS FROM GREAT FINDS

A wide variety of objects can be used for creative window treatments, from the necessary hardware to the curtains themselves. Let your interests and your decorating style guide you as you look through antique stores, salvage yards, flea markets, or even your own attic. Consider yokes and metal spurs for Western or country decorating. If boating is your favorite pastime, use an old oar, perhaps with fishing tackle and a fish net. A sports fan, on the other hand, might choose old pennants, used as a valance.

Boat oar *serves as a rustic curtain rod for a swagged window treatment.*

Metal spurs *(left) become tieback holders for a Western decorating style.*

Screw metal spurs directly to the wall through the holes in the spurs.

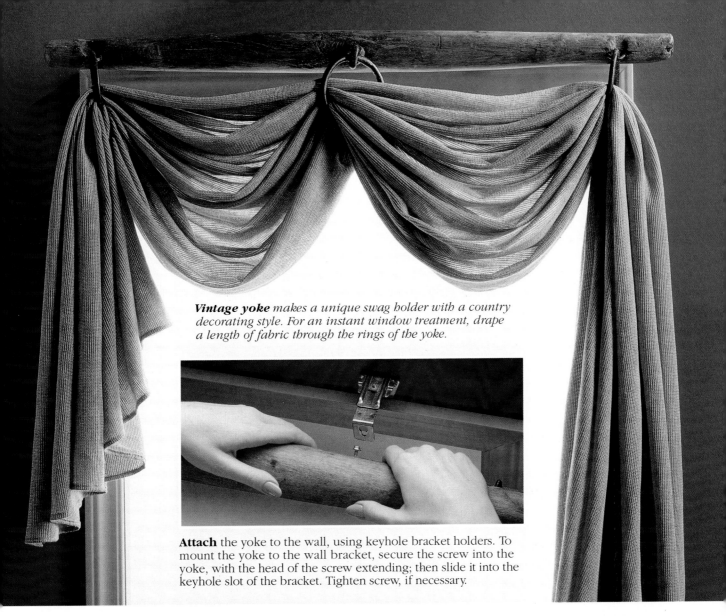

Vintage yoke *makes a unique swag holder with a country decorating style. For an instant window treatment, drape a length of fabric through the rings of the yoke.*

Attach the yoke to the wall, using keyhole bracket holders. To mount the yoke to the wall bracket, secure the screw into the yoke, with the head of the screw extending; then slide it into the keyhole slot of the bracket. Tighten screw, if necessary.

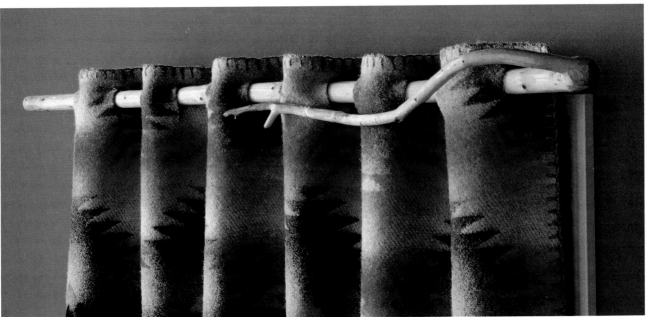

Walking cane, *attached with keyhole bracket holders as shown above, makes a creative curtain rod, and a wool blanket becomes the curtain. Thread the blanket onto the rod through slits cut along the top of the blanket.*

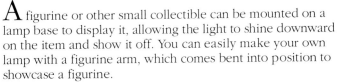

COLLECTOR'S LAMPS

A figurine or other small collectible can be mounted on a lamp base to display it, allowing the light to shine downward on the item and show it off. You can easily make your own lamp with a figurine arm, which comes bent into position to showcase a figurine.

Figurine arms are available at lighting repair stores in different heights, with the arms offset about 2½" to 3" (6.5 to 7.5 cm). Select the arm size that accommodates the size of the collectible you are displaying. If there is not enough threading on the lower end of the arm to accommodate the lamp base and the connecting lamp parts you are using (page 72), it may be necessary to have the pipe threaded at a lighting repair store.

The other necessary lamp parts are also available from lighting repair stores and hardware stores, including the special lamp bases designed for use with figurine arms. If you prefer, you can make your own lamp base cut from wood, drilling a ½" (1.3 cm) hole near the back of the base.

MATERIALS

- Figurine or other collector's item.
- Lamp base; self-adhesive base pad, optional.
- ⅛ IPS figurine arm; if necessary, have lower end of arm threaded to correct length (page 72) at a lighting repair store.
- ⅛ IPS hex nut and plastic cap nut.
- Fender washer; lock washer.
- Electrical lamp cord with wall plug.
- Socket with 3-way switch, or push-through switch for single-watt bulb.
- Brass neck.
- Clip-on lamp shade designed to attach directly to light bulb, or lamp shade with clip-on adapter.
- Finial.
- Drill and drill bit, if necessary for drilling hole into lamp base.
- Glue for securing collector's item to lamp base; type of glue depends on item used.
- Screwdriver; utility knife; wire stripper, optional.

Collectibles *like a brass elephant and old books (opposite) and a primitive wooden statue (right) are showcased on table lamps. The lamps are easily assembled, using figurine arms and other basic lamp parts.*

DETERMINING THE LENGTH OF THE THREADED PIPE

Determine the necessary amount of threading for the lower end of the figurine arm, based on the thickness of the lamp base and lower lamp parts you are using. Measure the combined thicknesses of the brass threaded washer, decorative brass washer, fender washer, one lock washer, hex nut, and the threaded portion of the plastic end cap (as shown stacked). Measure the depth of the hole in the lamp base, not including the recessed area on the underside; insert a dowel into the hole and mark it, to easily measure the depth of the hole. Add these measurements together to determine the length of the threaded pipe needed at the end of the figurine arm. An arm can be threaded to this length at a lighting repair store.

HOW TO MAKE A COLLECTOR'S LAMP

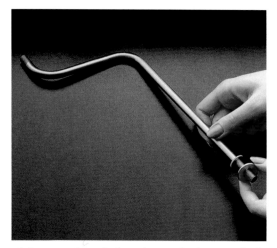

1 Screw a threaded washer to the base end of the lamp pipe as far as possible; then place decorative brass washer over end of lamp pipe.

2 Turn lamp base over. Insert end of lamp pipe up through lamp base. From underside of lamp base, place a fender washer, then a lock washer, onto the lamp pipe. Screw hex nut onto pipe; check to see that bend in lamp pipe is in correct position. Tighten hex nut. Screw on plastic cap.

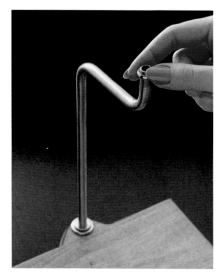

3 Screw threaded washer onto top of lamp pipe.

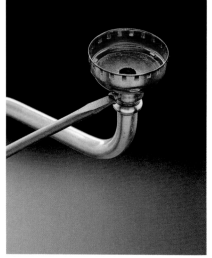

4 Loosen screw located on side of socket cap. Screw socket cap onto lamp pipe; tighten socket cap screw.

5 Tighten lock washer and threaded washer against socket cap.

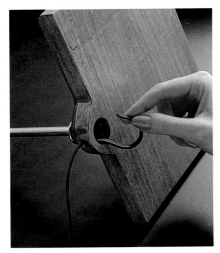

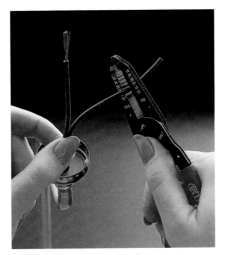

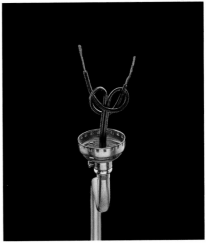

6 Insert electrical cord through hole in base and up through lamp pipe. If footed lamp pipe is used, insert cord directly through lamp pipe.

7 Split the end of the cord along the midline of insulation, using a utility knife; separate the cord for 2" (5 cm). Remove about ½" to ¾" (1.3 to 2 cm) of insulation from ends, using a wire stripper or knife.

8 Tie an underwriter's knot by forming an overhand loop with one cord and an underhand loop with the remaining cord; insert each cord end through the loop of the other cord.

9 Loosen the terminal screws on socket. Loop wire on *rounded side* of cord around gold screw; tighten screw. Loop wire on *ribbed side* of cord around silver screw; tighten screw. Make sure that all strands of wire are wrapped around the screws.

...

10 Adjust the underwriter's knot snug against base of the socket; position socket in socket cap. Slide insulating sleeve and outer shell over socket with terminal screws fully covered and sleeve slot aligned over switch.

11 Press socket assembly down into socket cap until the socket locks into place.

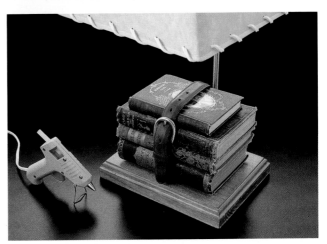

12 Secure self-adhesive base pad to bottom of lamp base, if necessary. Attach a clip-on lamp shade. Secure the collectible to lamp base, using an appropriate adhesive for the types of materials.

Lovely tiered trays can easily be made from china plates, using lamp parts for the spacers between the plates and for the decorative top finial. To insert the lamp parts, a center hole is drilled through each plate, using a special drill bit. You may drill the holes yourself or have them drilled for you at a lighting repair or glass supply store.

To drill through ceramic or glass, use a ceramic drill bit; or use a hollow circular diamond drill bit and a drill press. To help prevent fracturing the plate while drilling, place mineral spirits or water in the plate to act as a lubricant and cooling agent, and drill slowly. Keep in mind that there is still some risk of fracturing the plate; for this reason, do not use valuable or irreplaceable pieces.

Glass, ceramic, or porcelain plates may be used. For a two-tier tray, choose a larger plate, such as a dinner plate or charger, for the bottom plate, and a smaller salad or dessert plate for the top one. For a three-tier tray, select three plate sizes so the tiers are graduated from larger to smaller, bottom to top.

To eliminate the need for a lamp base on the tiered tray, select a bottom plate that has a recess on the underside of at least 3/16" (4.5 mm), created by a rim. This allows the necessary space for the washers that secure the bottom plate. If the plate you select does not have an adequate recess on the underside, secure a lamp base under the plate to keep the tray from wobbling.

HOW TO MAKE A TIERED PLATE TRAY

MATERIALS

- Two or three plates in graduated sizes.
- ⅜" ceramic drill bit; or ⅜" hollow circular diamond drill bit and drill press.
- Lamp base, hex nut, and fender washer, if bottom plate does not have a recess of at least ³⁄₁₆" (4.5 mm) on underside.
- One threaded ¾" (2 cm) washer, if tray does not need a lamp base.
- Two ¾" (2 cm) rubber washers with ⁷⁄₁₆" (1.2 cm) center holes, for a two-tier tray; three rubber washers, for a three-tier tray.

- Two 1" (2.5 cm) brass washers with ⁷⁄₁₆" (1.2 cm) center holes, for a two-tier tray; three brass washers, for a three-tier tray.
- Three nipples, or threaded pipe, 1" (2.5 cm) long, to fit ⅛ IPS lamp pipe for a two-tier tray; five nipples, for a three-tier tray.
- One pair of decorative spacers with a combined length of 5" to 6" (12.5 to 15 cm), for a two-tier tray; or two pairs, for a three-tier tray.
- One decorative spacer for the top of the tray.
- One ⅛ IPS lamp finial or one ¼-27 lamp finial with reducer; one nipple, ⅝" (1.5 cm) long.

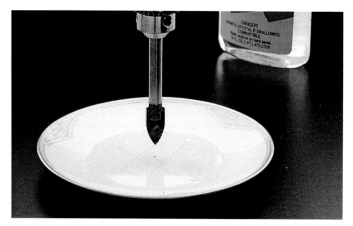

1 **Tiered tray without a lamp base.** Apply masking tape to each plate, centered on the front of the plate in an X; mark center. Pour mineral spirits into plate. Drill a ½" (1.3 cm) hole, using ceramic drill bit; drill slowly and keep the drill perpendicular to plate. Or drill hole with a hollow circular diamond drill bit and a drill press.

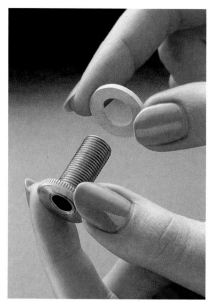

2 Screw a threaded washer to one end of a threaded nipple, so nipple does not extend beyond the threaded washer. Place rubber washer over other end of nipple.

3 Insert the threaded nipple into hole of bottom plate. Place 1" (2.5 cm) brass washer on the plate, over the nipple. Screw spacer onto nipple; do not overtighten, or the plate may crack.

4 Screw a threaded nipple into the top of first spacer; screw another spacer onto nipple.

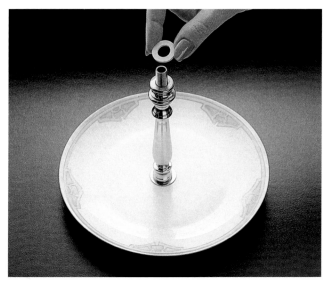

5 Screw another nipple into top spacer; place a rubber washer on top of spacer, over nipple.

6 Repeat steps 3 to 5 if making a three-tier tray, using a medium-size plate. Place the top plate over nipple and rubber washer; place brass washer on plate, over nipple.

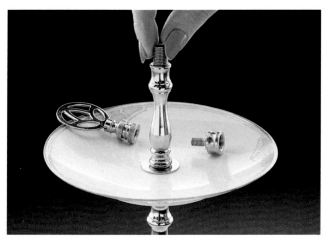

7 Screw on another spacer. Screw a nipple into spacer. Screw a reducer onto nipple, if ¼-27 lamp finial is used. Screw finial in place.

1 Tiered tray with a lamp base. Screw a hex nut onto one end of a threaded nipple. Place lock washer, then a fender washer over other end of nipple. Then insert nipple into hole of lamp base. Place a rubber washer on plate over nipple.

2 Complete tiered tray as in steps 3 to 7, opposite.

Found Fabrics

CLEANING OLD TEXTILES

Antique stores and attics often have a wide variety of old textiles, including linens, tapestries, handmade quilts, and needlework projects as well as christening gowns, wedding gowns, and other cherished garments. These textiles, whether used intact or made into pillows and other decorating accessories, add character and beauty to any decorating scheme.

When shopping for old textiles, look for pieces in good condition. If you are planning to cut apart a textile for use in a pillow or other decorating project, you may be able to work around any stains, holes, or weak areas. It may not be possible to remove stains from old fabrics, and, in the process of trying, you may even cause the fabric to disintegrate.

Because old silks are likely to be weighted with metallic salts, lead, and arsenic, handling them can be extremely hazardous. Old silk is so fragile, it is likely to tear, and, once torn, it releases harmful fibers.

There is certainly a risk involved in washing or dry cleaning old textiles, but knowing what precautions to take decreases the risk. Before cleaning old garments and quilts, repair any open seams and, if the item has any holes or weakened areas, reinforce the areas with a piece of net (page 87). Stitch around the outer edge of unfinished pieces, such as needlepoint canvases, quilt tops, or individual quilt blocks. It is not necessary to stitch around the selvages of tapestries.

Test the stability of the dyes before you decide to wash the fabric, as shown opposite. If the dyes bleed, dry cleaning is necessary; if no bleeding occurs, the fabric may be washed.

Keeping in mind that textiles are more fragile when they are wet, wash them gently by hand, using lukewarm or cool water and a small amount of mild soap. White or ecru textiles, such as laces, cottons, and linens, may need to be soaked for several hours to brighten them.

If dry cleaning is necessary and the textile is especially fragile, select a dry cleaner who uses the flat, rather than the tumble, dry cleaning method, because there is little abrasion with the flat method.

TIPS FOR CLEANING OLD TEXTILES

Wash old textiles (left) in a laundry sink or bathtub filled with lukewarm or cool water and a small amount of mild soap. Because fabric is more fragile when wet, lay the textile in soapy water and press against it with the palm of your hand, rather than agitating or wringing the fabric. For a heavily soiled item, change the washing solution often. Rinse several times; use distilled water for the final rinse.

Wash fragile items in pillowcase or mesh bag.

Lift a large textile item from the water, after washing it, using a piece of fiberglass screening that has been placed in the bottom of the washtub. This helps to prevent damage to the wet fabric. Prewash the screen to remove any oils, and bind the edges with tape.

Roll laundered textile in a white terry-cloth towel to remove the excess moisture; then air dry it flat on a plastic laminate surface or on a dry, white terry towel. A fan may be used to speed the drying process.

Test the stability of the dyes before washing a textile. Remove yarns of each color or small pieces of fabric from seam allowance or edge; or clip yarns from back of needlework. Lay yarns or fabric snips on white cotton, press with warm steam iron, and allow to dry for 10 minutes. If dye has bled onto white fabric, dry clean the textile instead of washing it.

Dry a tapestry or needlepoint piece faceup on plastic laminate surface, and gently pat it into its original shape. Place a layer of white cotton over the textile and press down on it with hands to remove excess moisture and speed the drying process.

DECORATING WITH OLD LINENS

The beautiful bed, kitchen, and table linens from years past proudly display various types of needlework, from embroidery to cutwork to handmade laces. Whether you own cherished heirlooms handed down in the family or just-found treasures from an antique store, these linens can add a special touch to your home decorating. An item that is stained may be arranged so the stains are concealed while it is on display. Or you can salvage the undamaged portions of the item to use for making pillows or other small accessories.

Unmatched tablecloths *in assorted prints are made into curtains, with clusters of artificial grapes used as tiebacks.*

Make a rod pocket at the top of the curtain panel, folding down the upper edge of the tablecloth **(a).** Or, if the tablecloth is too short to fold down the top, add a strip of fabric for the rod pocket **(b)** or for a facing at the upper edge **(c).**

Embroidered tablecloth is swagged elegantly over lace curtains. Raffia and a nosegay of preserved and silk floral materials are used as embellishments.

Vintage tea towel (below) is displayed in the bathroom over a terry hand towel.

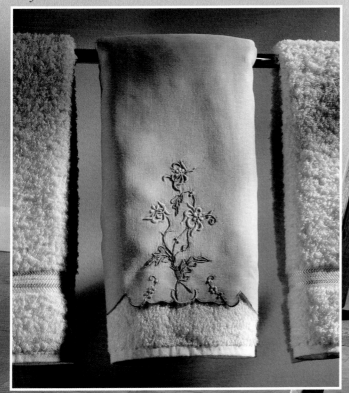

DISPLAYING & CARING FOR QUILTS

Old quilts have a nostalgic appeal. Regardless of the wear-and-tear they have received in the past, they continue to be appreciated for their handcrafted beauty. To help prevent deterioration, try these simple tips for displaying and caring for quilts.

To display quilts as wall hangings, stitch a fabric sleeve to the back of the quilt and insert a wooden lath into the sleeve. This distributes the weight of the quilt evenly. To protect the quilt from acids that could cause yellowing and disintegration, seal the lath with clear acrylic finish and use washed, unbleached muslin of 100 percent cotton for the sleeve. A sealed wooden or metal drapery rod can be substituted for the lath.

If the quilt design is not directional, turn the quilt every six months to reduce strain on the fabrics and stitching lines. Or take the quilt down after six months, perhaps replacing it with another quilt. This allow the fibers of the quilt to relax.

To prevent fading or fabric deterioration, display quilts away from direct sunlight or bright, constant artificial light, which speeds the fading and deterioration of the quilt. Select a low-traffic area, if possible, to reduce touching or handling of the quilt.

Store quilts at a humidity of 45 to 50 percent, to prevent stains from mold and mildew. Permanent creases are caused by folding and by pressure. When a quilt is folded for storage, the fibers along the folded edge are weakened and may break; the sharper the fold, the greater the damage. Putting weight on top of folded quilts increases the damage. For this reason, refold and restack stored quilts every six months.

Folded quilts in an open armoire make an attractive display.

Quilt wall hanging has a fabric sleeve stitched on the back, near the upper edge. A lath is inserted into the sleeve and then nailed or screwed to the wall.

HOW TO HANG A QUILT USING A FABRIC SLEEVE

1 Cut the lath ½" (1.3 cm) shorter than width of the quilt. Apply a clear acrylic finish to lath on all sides; allow to dry for 24 hours.

2 Cut a piece of washed, unbleached muslin of 100 percent cotton, 10" (25.5 cm) wide by the width of the quilt. At each end, turn under ½" (1.3 cm) twice; stitch to make a double-fold hem.

 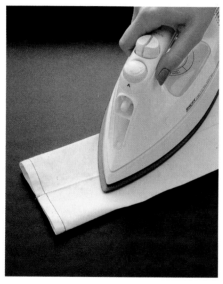 

3 Stitch long edges of the strip, right sides together, in ½" (1.3 cm) seam; press the seam open. Turn the sleeve right side out; press flat, centering seam.

4 Pin sleeve to back of quilt, close to edges. Hand-stitch sleeve to the quilt along the upper and lower edges; stitch through backing and into batting.

5 Insert finished lath through sleeve as shown below. Secure lath to wall, placing screws or nails at ends of lath.

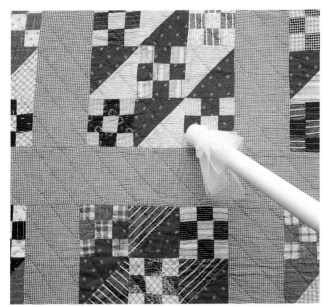

Vacuum displayed quilts often to prevent dust from causing the fabric to deteriorate. Secure a piece of net or the toe of nylon hosiery over the end of the vacuum cleaner hose, to keep quilt fabric from being drawn into the hose by suction.

Refold quilts that are folded, either for storage or display, using different foldlines each time, to prevent quilts from fading, wearing out, and becoming permanently creased on the foldlines. Refold quilts every six months.

Rotate quilts that are being stacked, from the bottom to the top, to prevent any permanent creases. If the stack is not rotated, the quilts on the bottom may become damaged along the foldlines from the weight of the other quilts.

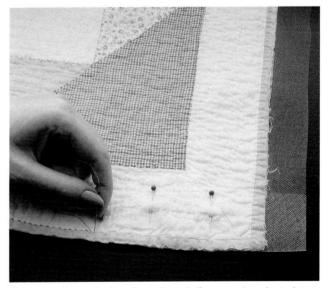

Cover surface of a fragile quilt with fine net, hand-stitching along seamlines, such as the seams between quilt blocks, sashing seams, and border seams. Wrap net to the back, around the binding; hand-stitch around quilt. If desired, a small area in poor condition can be covered with net, rather than covering the entire quilt.

THERE ARE NO
FARM GROWN GRAINS MILLDUST • FILLER
HUBBARD'S
SUNSHINE
SOW AND PIG
CONCENTRATE

FEED-BAG PILLOWS
WITH QUILT BORDERS

Feed bags and quilts are popular collectibles. Together, they make charming pillows. The feed bag works well as a creative inset, and the quilt can be cut into strips for the border. Use the remaining scraps from either the feed bag or the quilt for the back of the pillow.

Authentic old feed bags can be readily found at antique stores, and reproductions of the originals may be found at flea markets. Also available are seed bags and flour sacks, which work equally well for pillow insets. For the quilt border, it is not necessary to find a perfect quilt. A more affordable unfinished, damaged, or stained quilt may be used, because only a small amount of quilted fabric is needed.

A down pillow form is used to make this practical pillow especially soft and comfortable. A large pillow form, 22" to 28" (56 to 71 cm) square, is recommended, in order to feature both the printing on the feed bag and the piecework of the quilt. For best results, the feed-bag inset should measure about two-thirds of the pillow form. On 22" to 28" (56 to 71 cm) pillows, insets generally range from 14" to 18" (35.5 to 46 cm), with borders from 4" to 5" (10 to 12.5 cm).

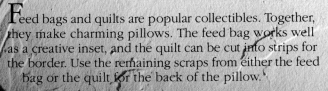

HOW TO MAKE A FEED-BAG PILLOW WITH A QUILT BORDER

MATERIALS

- Feed bag; seed bag or flour sack may be substituted.
- Quilt.
- Down pillow form.

CUTTING DIRECTIONS

For the feed-bag inset, cut a square of fabric from the front of the feed bag, 1" (2.5 cm) larger than the desired finished size of the inset; center the logo or printing from side to side and from top to bottom. The border strips and pillow back are cut during the construction process, in the following steps.

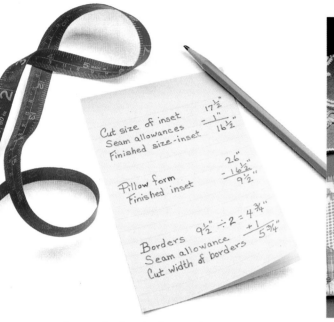

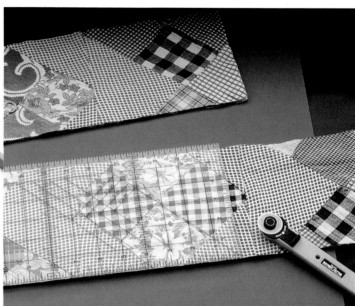

1 Subtract the finished size of the inset from the size of pillow form; divide this measurement by two. Then add 1" (2.5 cm) to determine the cut width of the border strips.

2 Cut two border strips from the quilt to the cut width determined in step 1; the cut length of the strips is equal to the cut width of the inset.

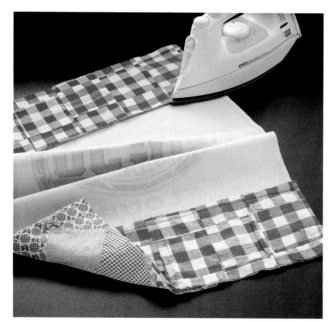

3 Stitch one border strip to the upper edge of inset, right sides together, stitching ½" (1.3 cm) seam. Stitch the second strip to lower edge of inset. Press seam allowances toward the inset.

4 Cut two remaining border strips from the quilt to the same cut width as previous border strips; the cut length of each of these strips is equal to the side measurement, including the borders.

5 Stitch one border strip to each side, right sides together, stitching ½" (1.3 cm) seams. Press the seam allowances toward the inset.

6 Use scraps from feed bag or quilt for the pillow back, piecing as necessary. Pin pillow front to pieced fabric for pillow back, right sides together. Using pillow front as a pattern, cut the pillow back.

7 Stitch ½" (1.3 cm) seam around pillow, leaving an opening on one side for turning; press seam open. At opening, press back the seam allowances. Trim corners diagonally.

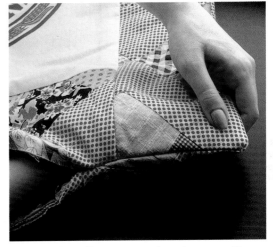

8 Turn the pillow cover right side out, pulling out the corners.

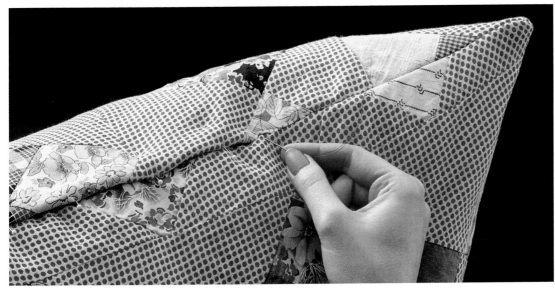

9 Insert the pillow form, pushing the corners of the pillow form into corners of pillow cover. Slipstitch the opening closed.

TAPESTRY PILLOWS WITH DECORATIVE TRIMS

Antique shops often have tapestries with exquisite designs. Even if a portion of the tapestry has been damaged or stained, the remainder can be salvaged. Transformed into luxurious pillows with decorative trims, these lovely tapestries make one-of-a-kind room accessories. The tapestry pillows featured here are made with a tapestry inset and a coordinating border fabric. Decorative gimp trims the border, and twisted cording, knotted at the corners, trims the outer edge.

Although the tapestry pillows have an opulent look, they are basicly sewn like the feed-bag pillows on page 89, with the tapestry insets measuring about two-thirds the size of the pillow form. To feature a pictorial scene in the tapestry, large pillow forms, 22" to 28" (56 to 71 cm) square, work best. In keeping with the luxurious quality of the fabrics, down pillow forms are recommended.

MATERIALS

* Tapestry, for the pillow inset.
* Coordinating fabric, for the border and pillow back, yardage varying with pillow size and fabric width; l yd. (0.95 m) is usually sufficient.
* Gimp trim; yardage is equal to twice the size of pillow form plus twice the size of inset plus 5" (12.5 cm).
* Decorative twisted cording, ½" (1.3 cm) in diameter, in cotton or rayon; yardage is equal to four times the size of pillow form plus 65" (165.5 cm) for the knotted corners.
* Down pillow form.
* Sewing machine needle in size 16/100.

CUTTING DIRECTIONS

For the tapestry inset, cut a square of fabric, 1" (2.5 cm) larger than the desired finished size of the inset; center the desired tapestry design from side to side and from top to bottom. To help visualize the look of the inset before cutting, place strips of paper around the design as shown below. The border strips and pillow back are cut during the construction process, on page 94.

Decide where to cut the inset from the tapestry fabric, using strips of paper to frame out the desired design area. Place the paper strips at right angles to each other, taping them together to leave a square opening of the desired finished size for the inset. Add ½" (1.3 cm) seam allowance on each side; cut fabric square.

HOW TO MAKE A TAPESTRY PILLOW WITH DECORATIVE TRIMS

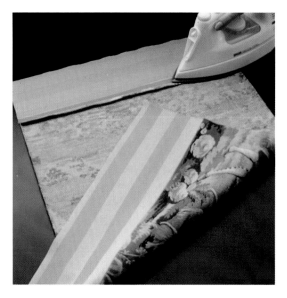

1 Determine the cut width of the border strips as on page 90, step 1. Cut two strips from the border fabric and stitch them to upper and lower edges of the inset as on page 90, steps 2 and 3; press the seams open.

2 Place gimp trim on pillow front, with gimp centered over seam at upper border; using size 16/100 needle, stitch in place along both edges of gimp. Repeat at lower border.

3 Cut remaining strips from border fabric and apply them as on pages 90 and 91, steps 4 and 5; press seams open. Stitch gimp trim over seams.

4 Pin pillow front to fabric for pillow back, right sides together. Using pillow front as a pattern, cut pillow back. Stitch and turn pillow cover as on page 91, steps 7 and 8.

5 Insert pillow form, pushing corners of pillow form into corners of pillow cover. Slipstitch opening closed.

6 Wrap and tie thread around the end of the cording, to prevent raveling. Hand-stitch the cording to one side of pillow cover, using running stitches; start with end of cording extended 1½" (3.8 cm) beyond corner.

7 Measure cording 16" (40.5 cm) beyond next corner; pin-mark cording at this point.

8 Continue stitching the cording around next side of pillow cover, starting at pin mark; leave loop of cording free at corner.

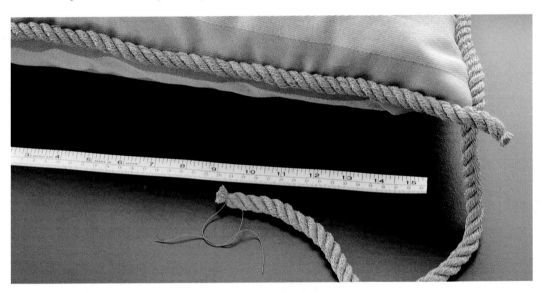

9 Repeat steps 7 and 8 for the remaining corners and sides of the pillow cover. At final corner, cut the cording 15½" (39.3 cm) beyond corner; wrap and tie thread around end of cording, to prevent raveling.

10 Overlap ends of cording ½" (1.3 cm). Hand-stitch through both ends of cording, and wrap thread tightly around the ends.

11 Knot cording at corners, close to the pillow. At final corner, conceal the overlapped ends of cording in the middle of the knot.

NEEDLEPOINT PILLOWS
WITH SHIRRING

An old piece of needlework, such as needlepoint, makes a decorative inset for a pillow. This round pillow has a shirred velvet border that complements the needlepoint and is trimmed with twisted welting.

If you select a twisted welting that twists in the opposite direction from the welting shown, interchange the use of the words "left" and "right" in steps 6 to 8.

The inset should measure about two-thirds the diameter of the pillow form. For example, for an 18" (46 cm) pillow form, the inset should be a 12" (30.5 cm) circle, and the finished shirred border should be about 3" (7.5 cm) wide.

MATERIALS

• Old needlework piece, such as needlepoint.

• Velvet or decorator fabric, for shirred border.

• Muslin.

• Decorative twisted weltings in ¼" (6 mm) and ½" or ⅝" (1.3 or 1.5 cm) diameters.

• Round pillow form.

CUTTING DIRECTIONS

Cut two circles from muslin, with the diameter of the circles ½" (1.3 cm) larger than the size of the pillow form; from the border fabric, cut the pillow back to this same size. Cut the needlework inset as in steps 1 and 2, opposite.

Cut the fabric strip for the shirred border, with the width 1½" (3.8 cm) larger than the desired finished width; this allows ½" (1.3 cm) ease for a softly shirred effect and two ½" (1.3 cm) seam allowances. The cut length of the border is equal to two times the circumference of the inset.

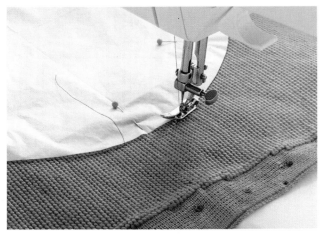

1 Cut out a circle from paper equal to the desired finished size of inset; place over needlework project, so circle is centered on the design from side to side and from top to bottom. Pin paper in place. Stitch around paper circle.

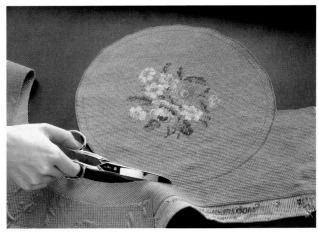

2 Stitch ½" (1.3 cm) outside stitched circle, using zigzag stitch, to prevent needlework from raveling. Cut inset just outside zigzag stitching, taking care not to cut stitches.

3 Center the inset piece on the muslin circle; pin in place.

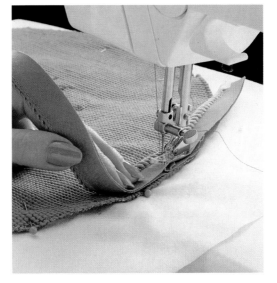

4 Identify right side of twisted welting; from right side, inner edge of tape is not visible. Baste the twisted welting to inset, right sides up, with cord along marked seamline, using zipper foot; leave 3" (7.5 cm) tail at beginning. Wrap transparent tape around the end of the tail to prevent raveling.

5 Leave 1" (2.5 cm) unstitched between ends. Cut welting, leaving 3" (7.5 cm) tail; wrap end with tape.

6 Remove the stitching from the welting tape on the tails. Trim the welting tape to 1" (2.5 cm) from stitching; overlap ends, and secure with tape. Arrange twisted cording with the cording at right turned up and the cording at left turned down.

(Continued)

7 Insert cording at right end under the welting tape, untwisting and flattening it under the welting tape as shown. Secure in place, using tape.

8 Place cording at left over cording at right until lapped area looks like continuous twisted welting; manipulate the cording as necessary, untwisting it partially to flatten it at seamline. Tape in place. Check the appearance on both sides of welting.

9 Machine-baste through all layers to secure the welting at the seamline; use zipper foot, positioned so you can stitch in direction of twists.

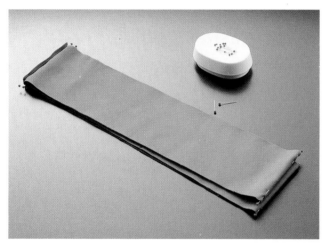

10 Seam the border strips together to form a tube. Fold into fourths, right sides together; mark both of the raw edges at folds.

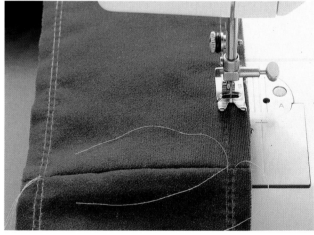

11 Stitch gathering rows a scant ½" and ⅜" (1.3 and 1 cm) from each raw edge of border strip, using long stitch length.

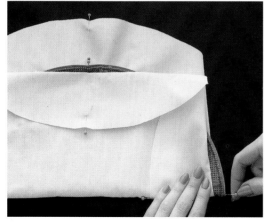

12 Fold pillow top into fourths; mark folds at outer edge of pillow top and at welting.

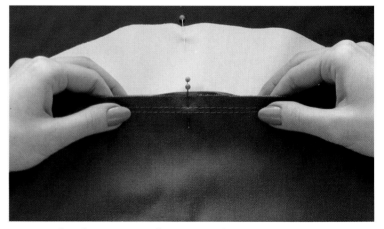

13 Pin border strip to pillow top, right sides together, with raw edge of border strip even with outer edge of needlepoint inset, matching markings.

14 Pull gathering threads, and distribute the gathers evenly; pin in place. Stitch, using zipper foot.

15 Pin outer edge of border to outer edge of muslin, right sides up, matching the markings. Pull gathering thread, distribute gathers evenly, and pin. Machine-baste gathered border to muslin.

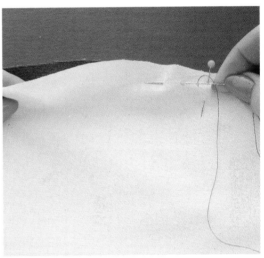

16 Stitch twisted welting to outer edge as in steps 4 to 9, with the right side of welting toward the right side of pillow top.

17 Hand-baste the remaining muslin circle to the wrong side of the pillow back.

19 Insert pillow form. Fold under edge; pin and slipstitch the opening closed.

18 Pin pillow back to pillow top, right sides together. Stitch ½" (1.3 cm) seam, leaving an opening for turning. Turn right side out.

MORE IDEAS FOR FOUND FABRICS

Antique garments *(above) are hung on a clothesline near the ceiling, for a creative bedroom display.*

Tapestry wall hanging *is sewn following the instructions for the tapestry pillow cover on pages 93 to 95. After the front and back are stitched together and turned, simply press the edges flat.*

Small purses, each handcrafted with beading or needlework, are displayed as a wall grouping.

Vintage kimono (right) is hung on a dowel, creating a simple, yet dramatic, wall display.

*Displaying
Great Finds*

DISPLAYING OLD PHOTOGRAPHS & DOCUMENTS

Old photographs and documents are often cherished for their historic or sentimental appeal. Today, there is increasing interest in preserving and displaying family photographs and documents that give an account of one's ancestral history, as well as in collecting vintage postcards, artwork, and news clippings.

Photographs and documents can be matted and framed for a traditional look. Or they can simply be attached to a mounting board and then framed without a mat; this is sometimes referred to as top mounting. To make sure that cherished items can be handed down from generation to generation, frame the items using the techniques for conservation framing. With conservation framing, the materials and procedures used help protect photographs and documents from atmospheric acidity and sunlight and allow for expansion during periods of high humidity.

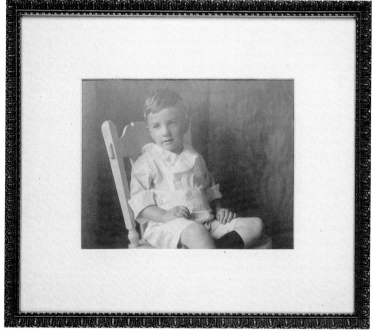

Cherished photograph *(above) is hinge-mounted with a bevel-cut mat. Opposite, a document over 100 years old is hinge-mounted without a mat, which allows the torn edges to show.*

While true conservation framing, or museum mounting, requires specialty materials and the skills of an expert, there are many precautions you can take when framing items yourself.

To protect photographs and documents from acids that cause yellowing and disintegration, use acid-free mat boards and mounting boards. Although regular mat and mounting boards are buffered to neutralize the acid in the wood pulp, purchase conservation-quality boards made from 100 percent cotton rag for maximum protection. To seal the acids that are in the wooden frame, apply a clear acrylic finish to the raw wood of the frame. To best preserve the framed item, use UV-protective glass. This glass is more expensive than standard glass, but provides protection from 95 percent of the sun's damaging ultraviolet rays.

To avoid trapping moisture against the photograph or the document, it is important to allow air space under the glass. When you are not matting the photograph, use spacers to keep the glass from touching it. Narrow plastic strips, designed with a channel that fits over the edge of the glass, are available from framing stores. The spacers can be cut to the length of the glass.

Gummed linen framer's tape is the preferred tape for mounting, because it is acid free. Acid-neutral double-stick transfer tape, or adhesive transfer gum (ATG) tape, may be used to attach the paper dustcover to the back of the frame.

Mats are easy to cut using a mat cutter with a 45° beveled edge. Mat cutters come in a variety of styles and prices. For best results, select one that has a retractable blade and is marked with a start-and-stop line. This line acts as a guide, making it easier to cut perfect corners. Specific cutting instructions may vary with the type of mat cutter.

- Acid-free mounting board.
- Acid-free mat board and mat cutter, for mounting a picture with a mat.
- 1" (2.5 cm) gummed linen framer's tape, for hinge mounting.
- Utility knife; cork-backed metal straightedge.

HOW TO BEVEL-CUT A MAT

1 Determine the size to cut the mat board by subtracting ⅛" (3 mm) from the dimensions of the frame opening; mark the wrong side of mat board, making sure the corners are square. Using a utility knife and a straightedge, score repeatedly along the marked line until board is cut through.

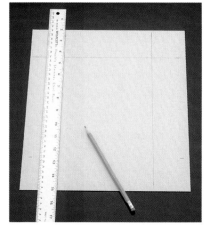

2 Mark width of mat borders, measuring from each edge and making two marks on each side; image opening should be at least ⅛" (3 mm) smaller than the photograph or document. Using sharp pencil and straightedge, draw lines connecting marks; extend lines almost to edge of the board.

3 Place a scrap of mat board under the area to be cut. Using a straightedge, align the edge of the mat cutter with the marked line, placing the start-and-stop line (arrow) of cutter even with upper border line.

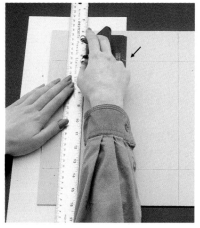

4 Push the blade into mat. Cut on the marked line in one smooth pass; stop when the start-and-stop line (arrow) meets lower border line. Pull blade out of mat. Repeat to cut remaining sides.

HOW TO HINGE-MOUNT A PHOTOGRAPH OR DOCUMENT WITH A MAT

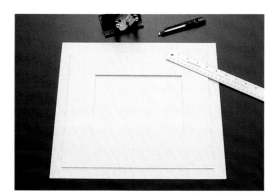

1 Bevel-cut mat board, above. Cut mounting board about 2" (5 cm) larger than mat board.

2 Cut a 2¼" (6 cm) strip of linen framer's tape; moisten ¼" to ½" (6 mm to 1.3 cm) at one end of the strip, depending on weight of the photograph or document; secure at upper edge on back of the photograph or document as shown, positioning the tape near one end. Repeat at the opposite end.

3 Place photograph faceup on mounting board in the desired position. Moisten and secure a 2" (5 cm) strip of tape directly along edge of photograph and perpendicular to first strip of tape. Repeat at opposite end.

4 Fold remainder of first strip over second strip; moisten tape, and secure.

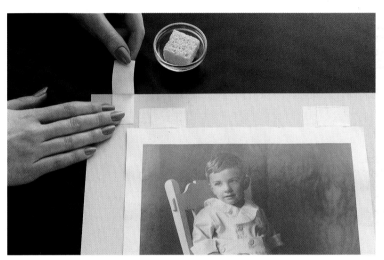

5 Place mat board over mounting board, with photograph positioned correctly in opening of mat; mark along outer edges of mat, using a pencil. Cut mounting board on marked lines.

6 Fold 3" (7.5 cm) strip of linen framer's tape in half, gummed side out. Moisten underside of strip; secure to mounting board, about 1" (2.5 cm) from end, with folded edge of strip directly along upper edge of mounting board. Repeat at opposite end.

7 Moisten the upper side of each strip, and position the mat on the mounting board, aligning edges; press to secure mat to tape.

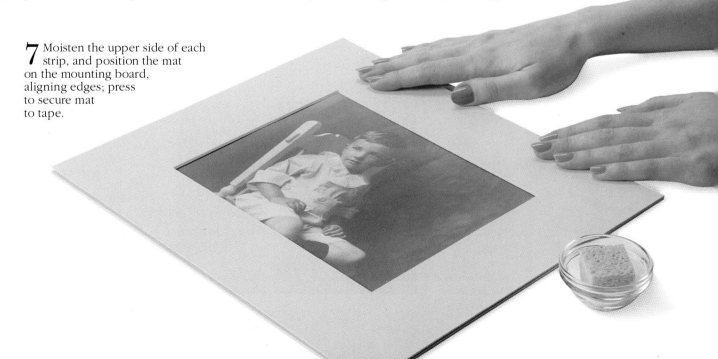

HOW TO HINGE-MOUNT A PHOTOGRAPH
OR DOCUMENT WITHOUT A MAT

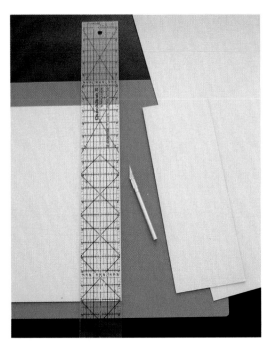

2 Fold ¼" (3.2 cm) strip of linen framer's tape, gummed side out, folding back ¼" to ½" (6 mm to 1.3 cm), depending on the size and weight of the document or photograph. Place document facedown on smooth, clean surface. Moisten short side of strip and secure to document as shown, positioned near one end, with the folded edge of the strip a scant ⅛" (3 mm) below upper edge of document. Repeat at opposite end.

1 Determine size to cut the mounting board by subtracting ⅛" (3 mm) from the dimensions of frame opening; mark wrong side of mounting board, making sure corners are square. Using a utility knife and straightedge, score along marked line; repeat until board is cut through.

3 Moisten the remainder of strip; secure to mounting board, positioning the document as desired.

HOW TO ASSEMBLE A PHOTOGRAPH
OR DOCUMENT IN A WOODEN FRAME

MATERIALS

- Wooden picture frame and glass; clear acrylic finish, for sealing raw wood of frame.
- Plastic spacers with channels for glass, for assembling a picture without a mat.
- ¾" (2 cm) brads, for attaching frame.
- Framer's fitting tool or slip-joint pliers.
- Brown craft paper, for backing paper.
- Double-stick transfer tape, or ATG tape.
- Two small screw eyes.
- Self-adhesive rubber bumpers.
- Small awl; braided picture wire; masking tape.

1 Seal raw wood of the frame, using clear acrylic finish; allow to dry. Bevel-cut a mat (page 106), if desired. Hinge-mount document or photograph (pages 106 to 108).

2 Clean both sides of glass thoroughly, using glass cleaner and lint-free cloth. If frame is being assembled without a mat, cut plastic spacers, using utility scissors or pruning shears, to fit on each side of glass. Attach narrow channels of spacers to sides of glass, or, if using thick glass, attach wider channels; spacers should fit snugly.

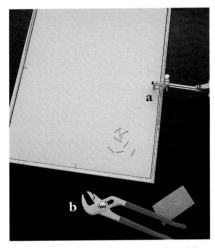

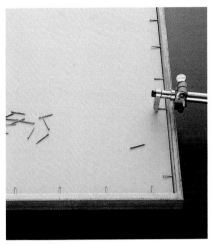

3 Position glass over document or photograph and mounting board, with edges even; if spacers are used, place the empty channels up. Position frame over glass. Slide fingers under mounting board; turn frame over.

4 Insert ¾" (2 cm) brads into middle of each side of frame, using framer's fitting tool **(a).** Or use slip-joint pliers **(b),** protecting outside edge of frame with strip of cardboard.

5 Recheck the face of the document for lint or dust; remove the brads and clean glass again, if necessary. Insert the brads along each side, 1" (2.5 cm) from corners and at about 2" (5 cm) intervals.

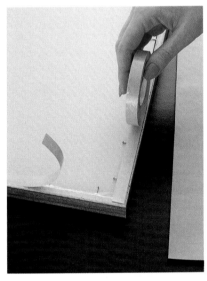

6 Attach double-stick transfer tape to the back of frame, about ⅛" (3 mm) from outside edges; remove paper covering. Cut the backing paper 2" (5 cm) larger than the frame.

7 Place paper on back of the frame, securing it to center of each edge of the frame and stretching the paper taut. Working from the center out to each corner, stretch paper and secure to frame. Crease paper over the outside edge of frame. Using a straightedge and utility knife, trim paper about ⅛" (3 mm) inside the creased line.

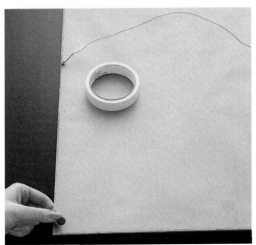

8 Mark the placement for screw eyes, using an awl, about one-third down from upper edge; secure screw eyes into the frame. Thread wire two or three times through one screw eye; twist the end. Repeat at opposite side, allowing slack; wire is usually about 2" to 3" (5 to 7.5 cm) from top of the frame when hung.

9 Cover ends of the wire with masking tape. Secure rubber bumpers to back of frame, at the lower corners.

Aged prints take on an elegant, Old World look when displayed in shirred fabric mats. This easy-to-make mat is made using double-stick framer's tape and does not require any sewing. The shirred mat may be used alone, or, to create a layered double mat with a shirred inner border, it may be used under a bevel-cut mat (page 106).

To make the shirred mat, wrap the fabric around a mat cut from mat board, gathering it in your hands as it is wrapped. The mat board can be easily cut to size, using a utility knife and a straightedge.

For best results, select a lightweight fabric, such as a silk shantung or handkerchief linen. The fabric strips can be cut on either the lengthwise or crosswise grain; however, on many fabrics, it is preferable to cut the strips on the lengthwise grain, for more controlled gathers. Before cutting, you may want to gather the fabric by hand to determine the best look for the fabric you have selected.

To prevent the glass from crushing the shirred fabric, spacers are used to lift the glass from the surface of the mat. Plastic spacers with a channel designed to fit over the edge of the glass are available from framing stores. For a layered mat with an inner shirred mat, spacers are not used, because the outer mat provides the necessary space between the glass and the shirred fabric border.

When using a shirred mat with prints that you want to preserve, such as those with monetary or sentimental value, refer to the information on conservation framing on page 104. To minimize the use of acidic materials, use an acid-free mat board and acid-neutral double-stick transfer tape, or ATG tape. Also select a fabric of 100 percent natural fiber, such as silk, cotton, or linen.

Shirred fabric mats *may be used alone, as shown above, or with a bevel-cut outer mat, opposite.*

HOW TO MAKE A SHIRRED FABRIC MAT
& ASSEMBLE THE FRAMED PICTURE

MATERIALS

- Lightweight fabric.
- Mat board; mounting board.
- Utility knife.

- Cork-backed metal straightedge.
- Double-stick transfer tape, or ATG tape.

- Materials listed on pages 106 and 108, for mounting and assembly, including plastic spacers.

1 Determine size to cut mat board by subtracting ¼" (6 mm) from the dimensions of the frame opening; mark wrong side of the mat board, making sure the corners are square. Using utility knife and straightedge, score mat board along marked line; repeat until board is cut through.

2 Mark the width of mat borders, measuring from each side; image opening should be at least ⅛" (3 mm) smaller than the picture. Cut the image opening in mat board.

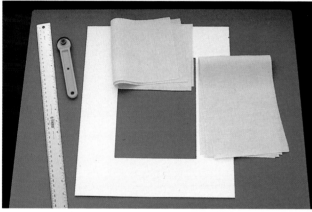

3 Cut a fabric strip for each side of the mat, with width of the strip equal to twice the width of the mat border; the length of the strip is equal to twice the length of the image opening.

4 Cut fabric squares for corner pieces, twice the width of mat border plus 2½" (6.5 cm); cut and discard 2½" (6.5 cm) squares from inner corners, to make L-shaped pieces as shown. Grainline should run in same direction on all corner pieces.

5 Place mat board facedown on table. Apply double-stick transfer tape to back of the mat board, along edges; remove paper backing.

6 Center a corner piece of fabric under the corner of the mat board. Wrap and secure the outer corner of the fabric to the corner of the mat. Wrap and secure the inner corner, creating gathers.

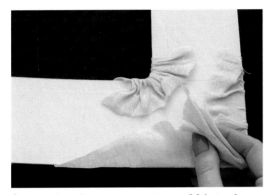

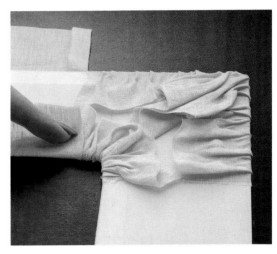

7 Hand-gather a corner piece of fabric along the inner edges; secure to the tape. Repeat along outer edges. Check appearance from right side; reposition as necessary.

8 Repeat steps 6 and 7 at the remaining corners. Fold under ½" (1.3 cm) along one short end of fabric strip for lower edge; wrap around mat, ½" (1.3 cm) from inner corner, and secure with strip of double-stick transfer tape.

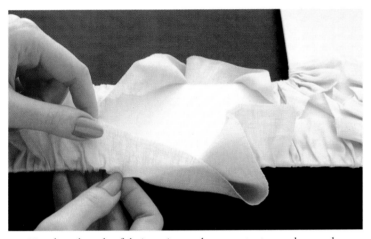

9 Hand-gather the fabric strip, and secure to tape along edges of mat board, working in sections. Fold under end of strip at opposite corner; secure with tape. Fabric may be repositioned on the tape as necessary for even distribution. Apply fabric strips to remaining sides of mat.

10 Hinge-mount the picture (pages 106 and 107). Assemble the picture in the frame (pages 108 and 109); use spacers as for assembly without a mat.

HOW TO MAKE A LAYERED MAT WITH A SHIRRED INNER MAT & ASSEMBLE THE FRAMED PICTURE

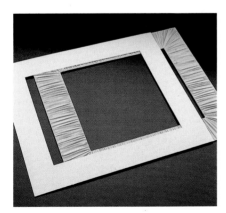

1 Make the shirred inner mat as in steps 1 to 9, opposite. From mat board, bevel-cut outer mat (page 106); cut the border ½" (1.3 cm) narrower than the shirred inner mat.

2 Hinge-mount picture (pages 106 and 107), using shirred inner mat as guide for cutting the mounting board in step 5.

3 Place the outer mat faceup over the shirred inner mat. Assemble the picture in frame (pages 108 and 109); spacers are not used.

Shadow boxes (above and right) display cherished family memorabilia.

DISPLAYING
MEMORABILIA
IN SHADOW BOXES

Showcase cherished mementos of the past in shadow boxes. These frames have deep sides that allow you to mount dimensional items, such as jewelry, watches, and other memorabilia. Shadow boxes are available in many styles and finishes and can be ordered in the desired size and depth at framing shops.

Foam-core board, wrapped with fabric, is used for the mounting board and to line the sides of the frame. For conservation framing (page 104), use acid-free foam-core board and natural-fiber fabric, such as 100 percent silk, linen, or cotton.

To determine the shadow box size you need, arrange all the objects to be framed on a sheet of craft paper, making sure to allow the desired amount of space around each item. Mark the frame size, and outline the items on the paper to record the placement. To determine the frame depth, measure the deepest item; add ½" (1.3 cm) to this measurement to allow for the frame assembly. Order the shadow box and the glass to these measurements.

Several methods may be used for mounting items. Photographs and documents can be hinge-mounted (pages 106 to 108), using linen framer's tape. Textile items, such as baptismal gowns and handkerchiefs, can be secured to the mounting board with small hand stitches. Many other items, such as earrings, lockets, and fishing poles, may also be secured with hand stitches. For inconspicuous stitches, use a thread that matches the item. Monofilament fishing line also works well for many items and is strong.

Lightweight items that cannot be stitched in place, such as plates, may be secured with clear silicone glue, available at hardware stores. This glue stays flexible and can be removed without damaging the item. Plastic clips designed for mounting items are available at framing stores in several sizes and styles to hold a variety of objects, including plates, pipes, coins, spoons, and fishing poles.

HOW TO MAKE A SHADOW BOX DISPLAY

MATERIALS

- Wooden shadow box.
- Natural-fiber fabric, such as 100 percent silk, linen, or cotton.
- ¼" (6 mm) acid-free foam-core board.
- Double-stick framer's tape, or ATG tape.
- Gummed linen framer's tape.
- Clear acrylic finish; paintbrush.
- Utility knife; cork-backed metal straightedge.
- Needle; thimble; thread; fishing line; clear silicone glue; or plastic mounting clips, such as Mighty Mounts™, as needed for mounting various items.

1 Seal unfinished wood of shadow box, using clear acrylic finish; allow to dry. Place glass in shadow box.

2 Mark strip of foam-core board ⅛" (3 mm) shorter and ⅜" (1 cm) shallower than inside top dimensions of the shadow box. Score repeatedly on marked lines, using utility knife and straightedge, until board is cut through. Repeat to cut strip for inside bottom.

3 Cut fabric 2" (5 cm) larger than each strip of foam-core board. Secure double-stick framer's tape to the foam-core board along all the outer edges. Center foam-core board, tape side up, on wrong side of fabric. Wrap fabric firmly around the long sides; press in place onto tape.

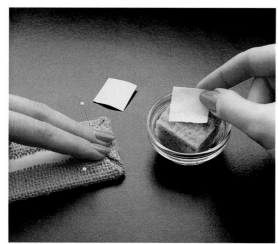

4 Wrap the fabric around ends, folding mitered corners; secure to tape. Secure the folded fabric at the corners, using moistened strips of linen framer's tape.

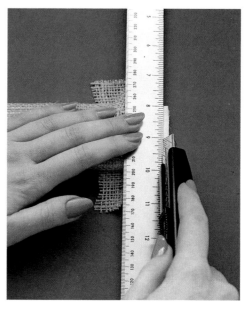

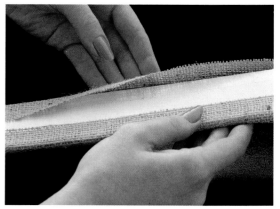

5 Position top and bottom pieces in frame; pieces should fit snugly without buckling. Repeat steps 2 to 4 for the side pieces. Check the fit of all pieces. If necessary, adjust size of pieces by peeling back fabric, then trimming the foam-core board and rewrapping it.

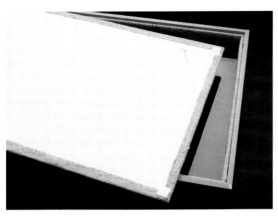

6 Cut mounting board ¼" (6 mm) smaller than the frame opening dimensions. Wrap mounting board with fabric as for side pieces. Check fit of mounting board; adjust, if necessary.

7 Remove the glass and clean it on both sides thoroughly, using a glass cleaner and a lint-free cloth. Reposition glass in frame. Cut strips of double-stick framer's tape; secure to back of each piece for sides of frame. Secure top and bottom pieces to frame, then side pieces.

8 Attach the items to the mounting board (below); attach photographs, if desired, as for mounting without a mat (page 108).

9 Place mounting board in frame. Recheck the display and glass for lint or dust. Complete the frame assembly as on page 109, steps 4 to 9.

TIPS FOR MOUNTING ITEMS IN A SHADOW BOX

Hand stitches. Arrange the item on mounting board. Determine several locations where article can be supported with small stitches. Thread a needle with monofilament fishing line or thread that matches item. Using threaded needle and thimble, secure item, taking about three stitches through mounting board at each support location. From back of board, tie the thread tails, and secure them to board with linen framer's tape.

Clear silicone glue. Secure any lightweight items with a bead of clear silicone glue. Allow the glue to cure for 24 hours before placing backing board into frame.

Plastic clips. Mark the location for holder. Punch hole to the back side of mounting board, using an awl. Insert the holder, and press speed nut into place. Trim the post a scant ⅛" (3 mm) from nut, using utility scissors or pruning shears.

DISPLAYING OLD ARTWORK IN CLIP FRAMES

Clip frames are ideal for displaying old artwork or news clippings because the simplicity of the frames allows the artwork itself to show off. Clip frames work well for any decorating scheme, but especially for modern interiors. Essentially, each frame consists of a piece of glass with a tension-mounted backing board. Clip frames are available from craft stores, art stores, and framing supply stores.

To enhance the artwork, you may add creative touches like irregular hand stitches, woven lengths of raffia, or pressed flowers. As a background for the framed objects, use a sheet of mat board or art paper. Keep in mind that the available mounting depth is limited by the frame's mounting brackets. Therefore, if dimensional items are used for embellishments, avoid using mat board or other heavyweight paper for the background.

Clip frames, readily available at craft stores, art stores, and framing supply stores, are easily assembled. First, secure the artwork to a sheet of art paper or mat board. Then, lay the artwork and the backing board facedown on the glass, and slide the clips in place.

Old print (below) is secured to a textured paper with hand stitches. Metallic thread is used.

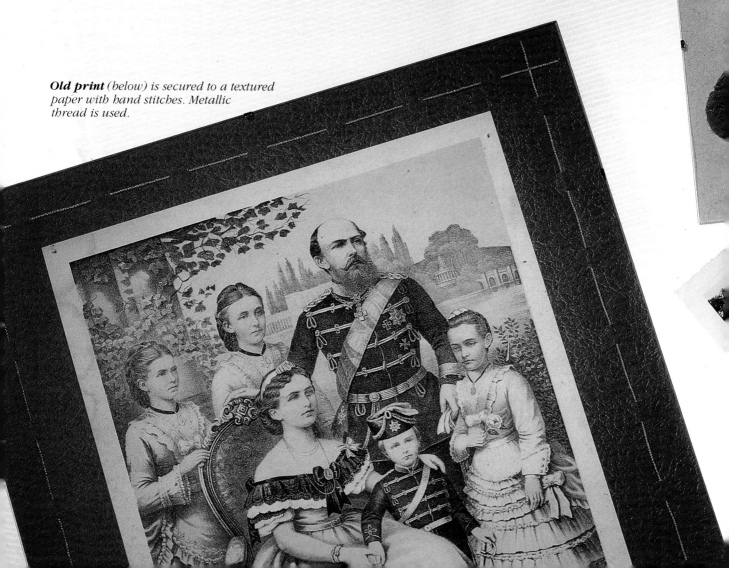

Old magazine advertisement (right) mounted on handmade paper makes an eye-catching piece of artwork.

Old family photographs (above) are arranged in a grouping with pressed flowers and a lace doily.

Old postcard (right) is mounted on rice paper with a cedar sprig and birch bark as accents.

Call for Life Savers...
say "hello" to refresh-mint!

PEP·O·MINT
LIFE SAVERS

with the hole

still only 5¢

Greetings from the
REDWOODS

COLLECTIONS

Escutcheons, *once used to add ornamental detail around doorknobs, are arranged in an organized fashion on a wall.*

If you are intrigued by antique jewelry or simply cannot resist handmade quilts, you may already be well on your way to establishing an impressive collection. While some people collect pieces within a broad category, such as figurines, others narrowly focus their collections to include items from a certain period, such as figurines from the late 1800s, or of a specific material, like porcelain figurines.

Collections on display can add character and personality to your decorating scheme and become a conversation piece for guests. Group the pieces together to maximize their impact.

Birdhouses and quilts, *both popular collectibles, are displayed in close proximity for more impact.*

Antique shoes are filled with dried flowers, creating a unique tabletop arrangement.

GREAT FINDS FOR DINING

Antique dinnerware pieces are appreciated for their elegance and often become collectibles displayed in china cabinets and on plate rails. Rather than keeping these items for display, you can feature them in a table setting.

Unmatched plates, goblets, and silverware are often more interesting than complete sets, so enjoy the freedom of mixing dinnerware styles. Used at the dinner table, these antique pieces can be combined with old linens for a truly nostalgic look. Or mix them with current dinnerware and linens, for an eclectic look.

Ornamental items (left) can be either glued or stitched to rings to create specialty napkin holders.

Salt and pepper shakers (right), each set unique in style, can be placed at every place setting.

Unmatched pieces (left) can be used together to utilize the single items you have collected.

Vintage table linens can have nostalgic appeal. Shown at right, tablecloths from the 1950s have been sewn into placemats, as for the wall hanging on page 100.

MORE IDEAS
FOR DISPLAYING
GREAT FINDS

Old wheelbarrow *serves as a creative magazine rack.*

Decorative bracket *becomes an important part of a wall grouping.*

Well-traveled suitcases *(left), stacked for use as an end table, are reminiscent of faraway places.*

Primitive masks *become an unusual wall display.*

Place setting, *consisting of vintage dishes, silverware, and linens, is mounted on a kitchen wall, creating a conversation piece. The pieces are glued together with silicone glue and then hung from a plate hanger.*

Exit signs *(right), found at antique stores, are displayed for nostalgic appeal.*

INDEX

CREDITS

CY DECOSSE INCORPORATED

A COWLES MAGAZINES COMPANY

Chairman/CEO: Bruce Barnet
Chairman Emeritus: Cy DeCosse
President/COO: Nino Tarantino
Executive V. P./Editor-in-Chief:
   William B. Jones

DECORATING WITH GREAT FINDS
Created by: The Editors of
   Cy DeCosse Incorporated

Also available from the publisher:
*Bedroom Decorating, Creative Window
Treatments, Decorating for Christmas,
Decorating the Living Room, Creative
Accessories for the Home, Decorating
with Silk & Dried Flowers, Decorating
the Kitchen, Decorative Painting,
Decorating Your Home for Christmas,
Decorating for Dining & Entertaining,
Decorating with Fabric & Wallcovering,
Decorating the Bathroom*

Group Executive Editor: Zoe A. Graul
Senior Technical Director: Rita C. Arndt
Senior Project Manager: Kristen Olson
Project Manager: Elaine Johnson
Associate Creative Director:
   Lisa Rosenthal
Art Director: Stephanie Michaud

Writer: Rita C. Arndt
Editor: Janice Cauley
Researcher/Designer: Michael Basler
Researchers: Linda Neubauer, Lori Ritter
Sample Production Manager: Carol Olson
Lead Samplemaker: Carol Pilot
Senior Technical Photo Stylist:
   Bridget Haugh
Technical Photo Stylists: Sue Jorgensen,
   Nancy Sundeen
Styling Director: Bobbette Destiche
Project Stylist: Coralie Sathre
Prop Assistant/Shopper: Margo Morris
Artisans: Arlene Dohrman, Sharon
   Ecklund, Phyllis Galbraith, Valerie Hill,
   Kristi Kuhnau, Virginia Mateen, Carol
   Pilot, Michelle Skudlarek, Nancy
   Sundeen
*Vice President of Development Planning
   & Production:* Jim Bindas
Director of Photography: Mike Parker
Creative Photo Coordinator:
   Cathleen Shannon
Studio Manager: Marcia Chambers
Lead Photographer: Mark Macemon
Photographers: Stuart Block, Rebecca
   Hawthorne, Kevin Hedden, Rex
   Irmen, William Lindner, Paul Najlis,
   Charles Nields, Mike Parker, Greg
   Wallace
Contributing Photographer: Brian
   Holman
Senior Publishing Production Manager:
   Laurie Gilbert

Desktop Publishing Specialist:
   Laurie Kristensen
Production Staff: Amy Berndt, Deborah
   Eagle, Kevin Hedden, Jeff Hickman,
   Jeanette Moss, Michelle Peterson,
   Mike Schauer, Greg Wallace, Kay
   Wethern, Nik Wogstad
Shop Supervisor: Phil Juntti
Scenic Carpenters: Rob Johnstone, John
   Nadeau
Consultants: Ray Arndt, Sr., Peter Basler,
   Corliss Forstrom, Kent Gebhard, Craig
   Mason, Larry Nelson, Barbara Sims,
   Gordon Wilcox
Contributors: Charlotte Ford Trunks;
   Conso Products Company; Dritz
   Corporation; EZ International; Kirsch;
   Plaid Enterprises; Swiss-Metrosene,
   Inc.
Printed on American paper by:
   Litho Inc. (0695)

Cy DeCosse Incorporated offers
a variety of how-to books. For
information write:
   Cy DeCosse Subscriber Books
   5900 Green Oak Drive
   Minnetonka, MN 55343